Low-Salt
Cookbook

Publications International, Ltd.

Pictured on the front cover *(clockwise from top left):* Three-Cheese Manicotti *(page 74),* Butternut Squash Soup *(page 46),* Peanut Butter Cereal Bars *(page 139)* and Apple-Cherry Glazed Pork Chops *(page 49).*
Pictured on the back cover *(top to bottom):* Mediterranean Pasta Salad *(page 43),* Mediterranean Pita Pizzas *(page 119)* and Banana Chocolate Cupcakes *(page 113).*

ISBN-13: 978-1-4508-4136-8
ISBN-10: 1-4508-4136-8

Library of Congress Control Number: 2011943398

Manufactured in China.

8 7 6 5 4 3 2 1

Nutritional Analysis: Every effort has been made to check the accuracy of the nutritional information that appears with each recipe. However, because numerous variables account for a wide range of values for certain foods, nutritive analyses in this book should be considered approximate. Different results may be obtained by using different nutrient databases and different brand-name products.

Microwave Cooking: Microwave ovens vary in wattage. Use the cooking times as guidelines and check for doneness before adding more time.

Note: This publication is only intended to provide general information. The information is specifically not intended to be a substitute for medical diagnosis or treatment by your physician or other health-care professionals about any medical question, diagnosis or treatment. (Products vary among manufacturers. Please check labels carefully to confirm that the products you use are appropriate for your condition.)

The information obtained by you from this publication should not be relied upon for any personal, nutritional or medical decision. You should consult an appropriate professional for specific advice tailored to your specific situation. PIL makes no representation or warranties, express or implied, with respect to your use of this information.

In no event shall PIL, its affiliates or advertisers be liable for any direct, indirect, punitive, incidental, special or consequential damages, or any damages whatsoever including, without limitation, damages for personal injury, death, damage to property or loss of profits, arising out of or in any way connected with the use of any of the above-referenced information or otherwise arising out of this use of this publication.

Publications International, Ltd.

Table of Contents

Breakfast

Potato and Pork Frittata

12 ounces (about 3 cups) frozen hash brown potatoes
1 teaspoon Cajun seasoning
4 egg whites
2 eggs
¼ cup low-fat (1%) milk
1 teaspoon dry mustard
¼ teaspoon black pepper
10 ounces (about 3 cups) frozen stir-fry vegetables
⅓ cup water
¾ cup chopped cooked lean pork
½ cup (2 ounces) shredded reduced-fat Cheddar cheese

1. Preheat oven to 400°F. Spray baking sheet with nonstick cooking spray. Spread potatoes on baking sheet; sprinkle with Cajun seasoning. Bake 15 minutes or until hot. Remove from oven. *Reduce oven temperature to 350°F.*

2. Beat egg whites, eggs, milk, mustard and pepper in small bowl. Combine vegetables and water in medium ovenproof nonstick skillet. Cook over medium heat 5 minutes or until vegetables are crisp-tender; drain.

3. Add pork and potatoes to vegetables in skillet; stir lightly. Add egg mixture. Sprinkle with cheese. Cook over medium-low heat 5 minutes.

4. Bake 5 minutes or until egg mixture is set and cheese is melted. Cut into four wedges. *Makes 4 servings*

Tip: If skillet is not ovenproof, wrap handle in heavy-duty foil.

Nutrients per Serving (1 wedge): Sodium: 258mg, Calories: 268, Calories from Fat: 37% Total Fat: 11g, Saturated Fat: 5g, Cholesterol: 145mg, Carbohydrate: 20g, Fiber: 2g, Protein: 22g

Banana Bran Bread

Banana Bran Bread

1 cup bran cereal
½ cup boiling water
1⅓ cups all-purpose flour
¼ teaspoon salt
1 teaspoon baking powder
½ teaspoon baking soda
¼ teaspoon ground cinnamon
2 eggs
⅓ cup sugar
2 tablespoons sugar substitute
2 tablespoons vegetable oil
1 cup ripe mashed bananas (about 2 medium bananas)
¼ cup crumbled unsweetened banana chips

1. Preheat oven to 350°F. Spray 9×5-inch loaf pan with nonstick cooking spray.

2. Place cereal in heatproof bowl; stir in boiling water. Let stand 10 minutes.

3. Meanwhile, combine flour, salt, baking powder, baking soda and cinnamon in medium bowl. Beat eggs, sugar, sugar substitute and oil in large bowl. Stir in flour mixture and bran; mix well. Stir in mashed bananas. Pour batter into prepared pan. Sprinkle with banana chips.

4. Bake 45 to 50 minutes or until toothpick inserted into center comes out clean. Cool in pan 5 minutes. Remove to wire rack; cool completely. *Makes 12 servings*

Variation: Fold in ½ cup dried fruit or sprinkle top of batter with chopped walnuts or pecans before baking if your diet plan allows.

Nutrients per Serving (one ¾-inch-thick slice): Sodium: 167mg, Calories: 135, Calories from Fat: 27%, Total Fat: 4g, Saturated Fat: <1g, Cholesterol: 35mg, Carbohydrate: 24g, Fiber: 2g, Protein: 2g

Super Oatmeal

Super Oatmeal

  2 cups water
2¾ cups old-fashioned oats
  ½ cup finely diced dried figs*
  ⅓ cup packed dark brown sugar
  ⅓ to ½ cup sliced almonds, toasted**
  ¼ cup flax seeds
  ½ teaspoon salt
  ½ teaspoon ground cinnamon
  2 cups reduced-fat (2%) milk
    Additional reduced-fat (2%) milk (optional)

Look for beige Turkish figs or use any variety of dried figs.

**To toast almonds, spread in single layer in heavy skillet. Cook over medium heat 1 to 2 minutes or until nuts are lightly browned, stirring frequently.*

1. Bring water to a boil over high heat in large saucepan. Stir in oats, figs, brown sugar, almonds, flax seeds, salt and cinnamon. Pour in milk.

2. Reduce heat to medium. Cook and stir 5 to 7 minutes or until oatmeal is thick and creamy. Spoon into individual bowls. Serve with additional milk, if desired.   *Makes 5 servings*

Nutrients per Serving (⅕ of total recipe): Sodium: 284mg, Calories: 380, Calories from Fat: 26%, Total Fat: 11g, Saturated Fat: 2g, Cholesterol: 8mg, Carbohydrate: 62g, Fiber: 9g, Protein: 12g

Pea and Spinach Frittata

Pea and Spinach Frittata

Nonstick cooking spray
1 cup chopped onion
¼ cup water
1 cup frozen peas
1 cup torn stemmed spinach
6 egg whites
2 eggs
½ cup cooked brown rice
¼ cup fat-free (skim) milk
2 tablespoons grated Romano or Parmesan cheese,
plus additional for garnish
1 tablespoon chopped fresh mint *or* **1 teaspoon dried**
mint leaves, crushed
¼ teaspoon black pepper
⅛ teaspoon salt

1. Spray large skillet with cooking spray; add onion and water. Bring to a boil over high heat. Reduce heat to medium; cover and cook 2 to 3 minutes or until onion is tender. Stir in peas; cook until heated through. Drain. Add spinach; cook and stir 1 minute or until spinach just begins to wilt.

2. Whisk egg whites, eggs, rice, milk, 2 tablespoons cheese, mint, pepper and salt in medium bowl; pour over vegetables in skillet. Cook without stirring 2 minutes until eggs begin to set. Lift edge of egg with spatula to allow uncooked portion to flow underneath. Remove skillet from heat when eggs are almost set but surface is still moist.

3. Sprinkle with additional cheese, if desired. Cover; let stand 3 to 4 minutes or until surface is set. Cut into four wedges.

Makes 4 servings

Nutrients per Serving (1 wedge): Sodium: 246mg, Calories: 162, Calories from Fat: 22%, Total Fat: 4g, Saturated Fat: 1g, Cholesterol: 110mg, Carbohydrate: 18g, Fiber: 4g, Protein: 14g

Sunny Seed Bran Waffles

Sunny Seed Bran Waffles

2 egg whites
1 tablespoon packed dark brown sugar
1 tablespoon canola or vegetable oil
1 cup fat-free (skim) milk
⅔ cup unprocessed wheat bran
⅔ cup quick oats
1½ teaspoons baking powder
¼ teaspoon salt
3 tablespoons sunflower seeds, toasted*
1 cup apple butter

To toast sunflower seeds, cook and stir in small nonstick skillet over medium heat about 5 minutes or until golden brown. Remove from skillet. Cool before using.

1. Beat egg whites in medium bowl with electric mixer until soft peaks form. Whisk brown sugar and oil in small bowl until well blended. Stir in milk.

2. Combine bran, oats, baking powder and salt in large bowl; mix well. Stir milk mixture into bran mixture. Add sunflower seeds; stir just until moistened. *Do not overmix.* Gently fold in beaten egg whites.

3. Spray nonstick waffle iron with cooking spray; heat according to manufacturer's directions. Stir batter; spoon ½ cup batter into waffle iron for each waffle. Cook until steaming stops and waffle is golden brown. Top each waffle with ¼ cup apple butter.

Makes 4 waffles

Note: It is essential to use a nonstick waffle iron because of the low fat content of these waffles.

Nutrients per Serving (1 waffle with ¼ cup apple butter):
Sodium: 318mg, Calories: 384, Calories from Fat: 23%,
Total Fat: 10g, Saturated Fat: 1g, Cholesterol: 1mg,
Carbohydrate: 68g, Fiber: 6g, Protein: 12g

Mixed Berry Whole Grain Coffee Cake

Mixed Berry Whole Grain Coffee Cake

1¼ cups all-purpose flour, divided
¾ cup quick oats
¾ cup packed light brown sugar
3 tablespoons butter, softened
1 cup whole wheat flour
1 cup fat-free (skim) milk
¾ cup granulated sugar
¼ cup canola oil
1 egg, lightly beaten
1 tablespoon baking powder
1 teaspoon ground cinnamon
½ teaspoon salt
1½ cups frozen unsweetened mixed berries, thawed
     and drained *or* 2 cups fresh berries
¼ cup chopped walnuts

1. Preheat oven to 350°F. Spray 9×5-inch loaf pan with nonstick cooking spray.

2. Combine ¼ cup all-purpose flour, oats and brown sugar in small bowl. Cut in butter with pastry blender or fork until crumbly.

3. Beat remaining 1 cup all-purpose flour, whole wheat flour, milk, granulated sugar, oil, egg, baking powder, cinnamon and salt in large bowl with electric mixer or whisk until well blended. Fold in berries. Pour into prepared pan. Sprinkle evenly with oat mixture and walnuts.

4. Bake 38 to 40 minutes or until toothpick inserted into center comes out clean. Cool in pan 5 minutes. Remove to wire rack; serve warm.   *Makes 12 servings*

Nutrients per Serving (1 slice): Sodium: 256mg, Calories: 272, Calories from Fat: 33%, Total Fat: 10g, Saturated Fat: 3g, Cholesterol: 26mg, Carbohydrate: 42g, Fiber: 3g, Protein: 5g

Scrambled Egg and Red Pepper Pockets

Scrambled Egg and Red Pepper Pockets

1 egg
2 egg whites
1 tablespoon fat-free (skim) milk
⅛ teaspoon kosher salt (optional)
⅛ teaspoon black pepper
  Nonstick cooking spray
1½ teaspoons unsalted butter, softened and divided
3 tablespoons minced red onion
2 tablespoons diced drained roasted red pepper
1 (6-inch) whole wheat pita bread round, halved and warmed

1. Whisk egg, egg whites, milk, salt, if desired, and black pepper in medium bowl until blended.

2. Spray medium skillet with cooking spray. Melt ½ teaspoon butter over medium heat. Add onion; cook and stir 3 to 5 minutes or until lightly browned. Add egg mixture; sprinkle with red pepper. Stir gently, lifting edge to allow uncooked portion to flow underneath. Continue cooking until set.

3. Evenly spread inside of each pita half with remaining 1 teaspoon butter. Spoon egg mixture into pita halves.   *Makes 2 servings*

Note: An ideal breakfast includes lean protein, complex carbohydrates, and a little bit of fat. This recipe includes all of these for a nutritious breakfast and it's filling enough to get you through the morning.

Nutrients per Serving (1 filled pita half): Sodium: 285mg, Calories: 155, Calories from Fat: 35%, Total Fat: 6g, Saturated Fat: 3g, Cholesterol: 113mg, Carbohydrate: 17g, Fiber: 3g, Protein: 8g

Breakfast Quinoa

Breakfast Quinoa

½ cup uncooked quinoa

1 cup water

1 tablespoon packed brown sugar

2 teaspoons maple syrup

½ teaspoon ground cinnamon

¼ cup golden raisins (optional)

Raspberries and banana slices (optional)

Milk (optional)

1. Place quinoa in fine-mesh strainer; rinse well under cold running water. Transfer to small saucepan.

2. Stir in water, brown sugar, maple syrup and cinnamon. Bring to a boil. Reduce heat; cover and simmer 10 to 15 minutes or until quinoa is tender and water is absorbed. Add raisins, if desired, during last 5 minutes of cooking.

3. Top quinoa with raspberries and bananas and serve with milk, if desired. *Makes 2 servings*

Nutrients per Serving (½ of total recipe): Sodium: 9mg, Calories: 233, Calories from Fat: 12% , Total Fat: 3g, Saturated Fat: <1g, Cholesterol: 0mg, Carbohydrate: 47g, Fiber: 4g, Protein: 6g

French Toast Strata

French Toast Strata

4 cups (4 ounces) cubed day-old French or Italian bread
3 ounces cream cheese, cut into ¼-inch cubes
⅓ cup golden raisins
3 eggs
1½ cups milk
½ cup maple syrup
1 teaspoon vanilla
2 tablespoons sugar
1 teaspoon ground cinnamon
Additional maple syrup (optional)

1. Spray 11×7-inch baking dish with nonstick cooking spray. Place bread cubes in even layer in dish; arrange cream cheese and raisins evenly over bread.

2. Whisk eggs in medium bowl until blended. Add milk, ½ cup maple syrup and vanilla; mix well. Pour egg mixture evenly over bread mixture. Cover; refrigerate at least 4 hours or overnight.

3. Preheat oven to 350°F. Combine sugar and cinnamon in small bowl; sprinkle evenly over strata.

4. Bake 40 to 45 minutes or until puffed, golden brown and knife inserted into center comes out clean. Cut into squares. Serve with additional maple syrup, if desired.   *Makes 6 servings*

Serving Suggestion: Serve with fresh fruit compote.

Nutrients per Serving (1 square): Sodium: 237mg, Calories: 287, Calories from Fat: 28%, Total Fat: 9g, Saturated Fat: 5g, Cholesterol: 127mg, Carbohydrate: 44g, Fiber: <1g, Protein: 8g

Quick Breakfast Blintzes

Quick Breakfast Blintzes

1 teaspoon unsalted butter
¼ teaspoon ground cinnamon
¼ teaspoon ground nutmeg
2 firm ripe Bartlett pears, peeled and cut into ½-inch cubes
1½ cups (12 ounces) reduced-fat ricotta cheese
1 teaspoon vanilla
3 teaspoons powdered sugar, divided
8 (8-inch) packaged thin crêpes
Additional ground cinnamon (optional)

1. Melt butter in large nonstick skillet over medium heat. Stir in cinnamon and nutmeg. Add pears; cook and stir 3 to 4 minutes or until warmed and tender.

2. Combine ricotta cheese and vanilla in medium bowl. Sprinkle 1 teaspoon powdered sugar on sheet of waxed paper or work surface. Place crêpes on paper and spoon ricotta cheese mixture down center of crêpes. Spoon pears over cheese; roll up and place on microwave-safe serving plates.

3. Working with two blintzes at a time, microwave on HIGH 20 to 30 seconds or until warm.

4. Place remaining 2 teaspoons powdered sugar in fine-mesh strainer; shake over blintzes. Sprinkle with cinnamon, if desired.

Makes 4 servings

Nutrients per Serving (2 blintzes): Sodium: 183mg, Calories: 231, Calories from Fat: 23%, Total Fat: 6g, Saturated Fat: 3g, Cholesterol: 35mg, Carbohydrate: 34g, Fiber: 4g, Protein: 10g

Sun-Dried Tomato Scones

Sun-Dried Tomato Scones

 2 cups buttermilk baking mix
 ¼ cup grated Parmesan cheese
 1½ teaspoons dried basil
 ⅔ cup reduced-fat (2%) milk
 ½ cup chopped drained oil-packed sun-dried tomatoes
 ¼ cup chopped green onions

1. Preheat oven to 450°F. Lightly grease baking sheet.

2. Combine baking mix, cheese and basil in medium bowl. Stir in milk, tomatoes and green onions just until dry ingredients are moistened. Drop by heaping teaspoonfuls onto prepared baking sheet.

3. Bake 8 to 10 minutes or until light golden brown. Cool on baking sheet 5 minutes. Remove to wire rack; serve warm.

Makes 18 scones

Nutrients per Serving (1 scone): Sodium: 197mg, Calories: 71, Calories from Fat: 38%, Total Fat: 3g, Saturated Fat: <1g, Cholesterol: 2mg, Carbohydrate: 10g, Fiber: <1g, Protein: 2g

Soups and Salads

Vegetable Beef Noodle Soup

Nonstick cooking spray
8 ounces beef for stew, cut into ½-inch pieces
¾ cup unpeeled cubed potato (about 1 medium potato)
½ cup sliced carrots
1 tablespoon balsamic vinegar
¾ teaspoon dried thyme
¼ teaspoon black pepper
2½ cups fat-free reduced-sodium beef broth
1 cup water
¼ cup chili sauce or ketchup
2 ounces uncooked thin egg noodles
¾ cup jarred or canned pearl onions, rinsed and drained
¼ cup frozen peas

1. Spray large saucepan with cooking spray; heat over medium-high heat. Add beef; cook 3 minutes or until browned on all sides, stirring occasionally. Remove from pan.

2. Reduce heat to medium. Add potato, carrots, vinegar, thyme and pepper to same saucepan; cook 3 minutes. Add broth, water and chili sauce. Bring to a boil over medium-high heat; add beef. Reduce heat to medium-low; cover and simmer 30 minutes or until meat is almost fork-tender.

3. Increase heat to high; bring soup to a boil. Add noodles; cover and cook 7 to 10 minutes or until noodles are tender, stirring occasionally. Add onions and peas; cook 1 minute or until heated through. *Makes 6 servings*

Nutrients per Serving (1½ cups): Sodium: 258mg, Calories: 182, Calories from Fat: 15%, Total Fat: 3g, Saturated Fat: 1g, Cholesterol: 28mg, Carbohydrate: 24g, Fiber: 1g, Protein: 15g

Mediterranean Artichoke Salad with Rotini

Mediterranean Artichoke Salad with Rotini

½ cup uncooked whole wheat rotini (about 1 ounce)

½ (14-ounce) can quartered artichoke hearts, rinsed, drained and coarsely chopped

4 to 6 medium button mushrooms, thinly sliced

½ medium tomato, chopped

¼ cup finely chopped red onion

8 kalamata olives, pitted and coarsely chopped

2 tablespoons snipped fresh parsley

1½ tablespoons white wine vinegar

½ clove garlic, minced

1 ounce crumbled feta cheese with sun-dried tomatoes and basil

1. Cook pasta according to package directions, omitting salt. Drain and run under cold water until pasta is cool. Drain well.

2. Meanwhile, combine artichokes, mushrooms, tomato, onion, olives, parsley, vinegar and garlic in medium bowl. Stir in pasta and cheese. Let stand 15 minutes for flavors to blend.

3. Serve immediately or cover with plastic wrap and refrigerate up to 4 hours. *Makes 4 servings*

Nutrients per Serving (½ cup): Sodium: 263mg, Calories: 111, Calories from Fat: 32%, Total Fat: 4g, Saturated Fat: 2g, Cholesterol: 5mg, Carbohydrate: 16g, Fiber: 2g, Protein: 5g

Chicken Barley Soup

Chicken Barley Soup

1 teaspoon olive oil
1 package (8 ounces) sliced mushrooms
¾ cup chopped onion
¾ cup chopped carrot
¾ cup chopped celery
2 cloves garlic, minced
4 cups fat-free reduced-sodium chicken broth
1 cup chopped cooked chicken
½ cup uncooked quick-cooking barley
¼ teaspoon dried thyme
¼ teaspoon black pepper
1 bay leaf
Juice of 1 lemon
Chopped fresh parsley (optional)

1. Heat oil in large saucepan or Dutch oven over medium-high heat. Add mushrooms, onion, carrot, celery and garlic. Cook and stir 5 minutes or until crisp-tender.

2. Add broth, chicken, barley, thyme, pepper and bay leaf. Bring to a boil. Reduce heat; cover and simmer 25 minutes or until vegetables are tender.

3. Discard bay leaf. Stir in lemon juice and sprinkle with parsley, if desired, just before serving. *Makes 8 servings*

Nutrients per Serving (1 cup): Sodium: 307mg, Calories: 102, Calories from Fat: 9%, Total Fat: 1g, Saturated Fat: <1g, Cholesterol: 13mg, Carbohydrate: 15g, Fiber: 2g, Protein: 9g

Garden Potato Salad with Basil-Yogurt Dressing

Garden Potato Salad with Basil-Yogurt Dressing

3 cups water

6 new potatoes, quartered

8 ounces asparagus, cut into 1-inch slices

1¼ cups bell pepper strips

⅔ cup plain low-fat yogurt

¼ cup sliced green onions

2 tablespoons chopped pitted ripe olives

1½ tablespoons chopped fresh basil *or* 1½ teaspoons dried basil

1 tablespoon chopped fresh thyme *or* 1 teaspoon dried thyme

1 tablespoon white vinegar

2 teaspoons sugar

Dash ground red pepper

1. Bring water to a boil in large saucepan over high heat. Add potatoes; return to a boil. Reduce heat to medium-low; cover and simmer 8 minutes. Add asparagus and bell peppers; cover and simmer 3 minutes or until potatoes are tender and asparagus and bell peppers are crisp-tender. Drain.

2. Meanwhile, combine yogurt, green onions, olives, basil, thyme, vinegar, sugar and red pepper in large bowl. Add vegetables; toss to coat. Cover and refrigerate at least 30 minutes or until chilled.

Makes 4 servings

Nutrients per Serving (¼ of total recipe): Sodium: 173mg, Calories: 154, Calories from Fat: 18%, Total Fat: 3g, Saturated Fat: 1g, Cholesterol: 2mg, Carbohydrate: 30g, Fiber: 3g, Protein: 6g

Mexican Tortilla Soup

Nonstick cooking spray
2 pounds boneless skinless chicken breasts, cut into ½-inch strips
4 cups diced carrots
2 cups sliced celery
1 cup chopped green bell pepper
1 cup chopped onion
4 cloves garlic, minced
1 jalapeño pepper,* seeded and sliced
1 teaspoon dried oregano
½ teaspoon ground cumin
8 cups fat-free reduced-sodium chicken broth
1 large tomato, seeded and chopped
4 to 5 tablespoons lime juice
2 (6-inch) corn tortillas, cut into ¼-inch strips
Salt (optional)
3 tablespoons finely chopped fresh cilantro

*Jalapeño peppers can sting and irritate the skin, so wear rubber gloves when handling peppers and do not touch your eyes.

1. Preheat oven to 350°F. Spray large saucepan or Dutch oven with cooking spray; heat over medium heat. Add chicken; cook and stir 10 minutes or until browned and cooked through. Add carrots, celery, bell pepper, onion, garlic, jalapeño, oregano and cumin; cook and stir over medium heat 5 minutes.

2. Add broth, tomato and lime juice; bring to a boil. Reduce heat to low; cover and simmer 15 to 20 minutes.

3. Meanwhile, spray tortilla strips with cooking spray; sprinkle with salt, if desired. Place on baking sheet. Bake 10 minutes or until browned and crisp, stirring occasionally.

4. Stir cilantro into soup. Ladle soup into bowls; top evenly with tortilla strips. *Makes 8 servings*

Nutrients per Serving (1¾ cups soup with tortilla strips): Sodium: 132mg, Calories: 184, Calories from Fat: 15%, Total Fat: 3g, Saturated Fat: 1g, Cholesterol: 58mg, Carbohydrate: 16g, Fiber: 4g, Protein: 23g

Broccoli Cheddar Salad

1 package (16 ounces) broccoli florets
¼ cup diced red onion
1 tablespoon cider vinegar
½ cup light mayonnaise
¼ cup (1 ounce) reduced-fat shredded Cheddar cheese
2 tablespoons raisins
2 tablespoons bacon bits
2 tablespoons sunflower seeds
¼ teaspoon black pepper

1. Bring large saucepan of water to a boil. Add broccoli; cook 15 seconds or until blanched. Drain and run under cold water until broccoli is cool. Drain well.

2. Combine onion and vinegar in small bowl. Let stand 1 to 2 minutes.

3. Combine broccoli and onion mixture in large bowl. Add mayonnaise, cheese, raisins, bacon bits, sunflower seeds and pepper; mix gently to combine. *Makes 6 servings*

Nutrients per Serving (1 cup): Sodium: 267mg, Calories: 127, Calories from Fat: 64%, Total Fat: 9g, Saturated Fat: 2g, Cholesterol: 12mg, Carbohydrate: 9g, Fiber: 2g, Protein: 4g

Fresh Tomato Pasta Soup

Fresh Tomato Pasta Soup

1 tablespoon olive oil

½ cup chopped onion

1 clove garlic, minced

3 pounds fresh tomatoes (about 9 medium tomatoes), coarsely chopped

3 cups fat-free reduced-sodium chicken or vegetable broth

1 tablespoon minced fresh basil

1 tablespoon minced fresh marjoram

1 tablespoon minced fresh oregano

1 teaspoon whole fennel seeds

½ teaspoon black pepper

¾ cup uncooked rosamarina, orzo or other small pasta

½ cup (2 ounces) shredded part-skim mozzarella cheese

1. Heat oil in large saucepan over medium heat. Add onion and garlic; cook and stir until onion is tender. Add tomatoes, broth, basil, marjoram, oregano, fennel seeds and pepper. Bring to a boil. Reduce heat; cover and simmer 25 minutes. Remove from heat; cool slightly.

2. Working in batches, purée soup in food processor or blender, returning blended soup to saucepan after each batch.* (Or use hand-held immersion blender.)

3. Bring soup to a boil. Add pasta; cook 7 to 9 minutes or until tender. Transfer to serving bowls. Sprinkle with cheese.

Makes 8 servings

Use caution when processing hot liquids in blender. Vent lid of blender and cover with clean kitchen towel as directed by manufacturer.

Nutrients per Serving (¾ cup soup with 1 tablespoon cheese): Sodium: 62mg, Calories: 116, Calories from Fat: 31%, Total Fat: 4g, Saturated Fat: 1g, Cholesterol: 4mg, Carbohydrate: 17g, Fiber: 2g, Protein: 5g

Pear and Cranberry Salad

Pear and Cranberry Salad

½ cup canned whole berry cranberry sauce
2 tablespoons balsamic vinegar
1 tablespoon olive or canola oil
12 cups (9 ounces) packed assorted bitter or gourmet
salad greens
1¾ pounds pears (about 6 small or 4 large pears)
2 ounces blue or Gorgonzola cheese, crumbled
Black pepper

1. Combine cranberry sauce, vinegar and oil in small bowl; mix well. (Dressing may be covered and refrigerated up to 2 days before serving.)

2. Arrange greens on six serving plates. Cut pears into ½-inch-thick slices; remove core and seeds. Arrange pears on greens and drizzle with dressing. Sprinkle with cheese and season with pepper. *Makes 6 servings*

Note: Be sure to use ripe pears. Forelles and Red Bartletts are particularly well suited for use in this salad.

Nutrients per Serving (⅙ of total recipe): Sodium: 165mg, Calories: 161, Calories from Fat: 34%, Total Fat: 6g, Saturated Fat: 2g, Cholesterol: 7mg, Carbohydrate: 26g, Fiber: 2g, Protein: 4g

Onion Soup with Pasta

Onion Soup with Pasta

    Nonstick cooking spray
    3 cups sliced onions
    3 cloves garlic, minced
    ½ teaspoon sugar
    2 cans (about 14 ounces each) reduced-sodium beef broth
    ½ cup uncooked small pasta stars
    2 tablespoons dry sherry
    ¼ teaspoon salt
    ⅛ teaspoon black pepper
    Grated Parmesan cheese (optional)

1. Spray large saucepan with cooking spray; heat over medium heat. Add onions and garlic. Cover and cook 5 to 8 minutes or until onions are softened. Stir in sugar; cook 15 minutes or until onions are very soft and browned.

2. Add broth to saucepan; bring to a boil. Add pasta; simmer, uncovered, 6 to 8 minutes or until tender.

3. Stir in sherry, salt and pepper. Ladle soup into bowls; sprinkle with cheese, if desired.   *Makes 4 servings*

Nutrients per Serving (¼ of total recipe): Sodium: 201mg, Calories: 141, Calories from Fat: 6%, Total Fat: 1g, Saturated Fat: <1g, Cholesterol: 0mg, Carbohydrate: 25g, Fiber: 2g, Protein: 8g

Mediterranean Pasta Salad

Mediterranean Pasta Salad

2 ounces uncooked bowtie pasta
1 cup canned chickpeas, rinsed and drained
1 cup canned artichoke hearts, rinsed, drained and quartered
¾ cup sliced zucchini, halved
¼ cup chopped red onion
3 tablespoons lemon juice
2 tablespoons olive oil
½ teaspoon Italian seasoning
⅛ teaspoon black pepper
⅛ teaspoon garlic powder
2 tablespoons crumbled feta cheese

1. Cook pasta according to package directions, omitting salt. Drain; run under cold water until pasta is cool. Drain well.

2. Combine pasta, chickpeas, artichokes, zucchini and onion in large bowl.

3. Whisk lemon juice, oil, Italian seasoning, pepper and garlic powder in small bowl until well blended. Drizzle over pasta mixture; toss to coat. Top with cheese before serving.

Makes 6 servings

Nutrients per Serving (⅙ of total recipe): Sodium: 142mg, Calories: 101, Calories from Fat: 27%, Total Fat: 3g, Saturated Fat: <1g, Cholesterol: 0mg, Carbohydrate: 16g, Fiber: 3g, Protein: 4g

Wild Rice and Asparagus Soup

Wild Rice and Asparagus Soup

½ cup instant wild rice

½ pound thin asparagus spears

1½ teaspoons margarine

1 shallot, minced *or* ¼ cup minced red onion

1 tablespoon all-purpose flour

1 cup low-sodium chicken or vegetable broth

½ cup fat-free half-and-half

¼ teaspoon crushed dried thyme

⅛ teaspoon black pepper

1. Cook rice according to package directions. Drain and set aside.

2. Meanwhile, trim asparagus. Place in large skillet with enough water to cover. Cook over medium-high heat 5 minutes or until tender. Drain. Cut into 1-inch pieces.

3. Melt margarine in medium saucepan over medium heat. Add shallot; cook 3 minutes or until tender, stirring occasionally. Stir in flour until absorbed. Stir in broth; cook 1 to 2 minutes or until slightly thickened. Add half-and-half, thyme and pepper. Stir in cooked rice and asparagus. Reduce heat to low; simmer 5 minutes.

Makes 4 servings

Note: If you prefer, you can cook regular wild rice instead of using instant. However, wild rice requires longer cooking than other rices. Avoid overcooking it because it will lose its characteristic chewy texture.

Nutrients per Serving (¾ cup): Sodium: 132mg, Calories: 199, Calories from Fat: 14%, Total Fat: 3g, Saturated Fat: <1g, Cholesterol: 9mg, Carbohydrate: 33g, Fiber: 4g, Protein: 9g

Butternut Squash Soup

2 teaspoons olive oil

1 large sweet onion, chopped

1 medium red bell pepper, chopped

2 packages (10 ounces each) frozen puréed butternut squash, thawed

1 can (10¾ ounces) condensed reduced-sodium chicken broth, undiluted

¼ teaspoon ground nutmeg

⅛ teaspoon white pepper

½ cup fat-free half-and-half, plus additional if desired

1. Heat oil in large saucepan over medium-high heat. Add onion and bell pepper; cook 5 minutes, stirring occasionally. Add squash, broth, nutmeg and white pepper; bring to a boil over high heat. Reduce heat; cover and simmer 15 minutes or until vegetables are very tender.

2. Working in batches, purée soup in food processor or blender, returning blended soup to saucepan after each batch.* (Or use hand-held immersion blender.)

3. Stir in half-and-half; heat through. Add additional half-and-half, if necessary, to thin soup to desired consistency.

Makes 4 servings

*Use caution when processing hot liquids in blender. Vent lid of blender and cover with clean kitchen towel as directed by manufacturer.

Serving Suggestion: Garnish with a swirl of fat-free half-and-half or a sprinkling of fresh parsley.

Nutrients per Serving (1½ cups): Sodium: **155mg**, Calories: **152**, Calories from Fat: **18%**, Total Fat: **3g**, Saturated Fat: **1g**, Cholesterol: **13mg**, Carbohydrate: **28g**, Fiber: **3g**, Protein: **6g**

Corn and Roasted Red Pepper Rice Salad

2 tablespoons plus 1 teaspoon canola or vegetable oil, divided
3 cloves garlic, minced
1 package (10 ounces) frozen corn, thawed
½ cup roasted red peppers in water, drained and chopped
2 cups cooked brown rice
¼ cup chopped fresh cilantro
¼ cup lime juice
1 tablespoon ground cumin

1. Heat 1 teaspoon oil in large skillet over medium heat. Add garlic; cook and stir 1 minute.

2. Add corn and peppers; cook and stir 1 minute or until heated through. Transfer to large bowl. Add rice and cilantro; mix gently to combine.

3. Whisk remaining 2 tablespoons oil, lime juice and cumin in small bowl. Add to rice mixture; toss to coat. Cover and refrigerate 1 hour before serving. *Makes 4 servings*

Nutrients per Serving (¾ cup): Sodium: **52mg**, Calories: **233**, Calories from Fat: **35%**, Total Fat: **9g**, Saturated Fat: **<1g**, Cholesterol: **0mg**, Carbohydrate: **35g**, Fiber: **4g**, Protein: **6g**

Main Dishes

Apple-Cherry Glazed Pork Chops

¼ to ½ teaspoon dried thyme
⅛ teaspoon salt
⅛ teaspoon black pepper
2 boneless pork loin chops (3 ounces each), trimmed of fat
  Nonstick olive oil cooking spray
⅔ cup unsweetened apple juice
½ small apple, sliced
2 tablespoons sliced green onion
2 tablespoons dried tart cherries
1 tablespoon water
1 teaspoon cornstarch

1. Combine thyme, salt and pepper in small bowl. Rub onto both sides of pork chops.

2. Spray large skillet with cooking spray. Add pork chops; cook over medium heat 3 to 5 minutes or until barely pink in center, turning once. Remove chops from skillet; keep warm.

3. Add apple juice, apple slices, green onion and cherries to same skillet. Simmer, uncovered, 2 to 3 minutes or until apple and onion are tender.

4. Whisk water and cornstarch in small bowl until smooth; stir into skillet. Bring to a boil; cook and stir until thickened. Spoon over pork chops.   *Makes 2 servings*

Nutrients per Serving (1 pork chop with ½ cup glaze):
Sodium: 191mg, Calories: 243, Calories from Fat: 30%,
Total Fat: 8g, Saturated Fat: 3g, Cholesterol: 40mg,
Carbohydrate: 23g, Fiber: 1g, Protein: 19g

Beef Stew in Red Wine

Beef Stew in Red Wine

1½ pounds beef round steak, cut into 1-inch cubes
1½ cups dry red wine
2 teaspoons olive oil
   Peel of ½ orange
2 cloves garlic, thinly sliced
1 bay leaf
½ teaspoon dried thyme
⅛ teaspoon black pepper
8 ounces fresh mushrooms, quartered
8 sun-dried tomatoes, quartered
1 can (about 14 ounces) fat-free reduced-sodium beef broth
6 unpeeled small red or new potatoes, cut into wedges
1 cup baby carrots
1 cup fresh pearl onions, outer skins removed
1 tablespoon cornstarch mixed with 2 tablespoons water

1. Combine beef, wine, oil, orange peel, garlic, bay leaf, thyme and pepper in large glass bowl. Cover and refrigerate at least 2 hours or overnight.

2. Place beef mixture, mushrooms and tomatoes in large nonstick skillet or saucepan. Add broth. Bring to a boil over high heat. Reduce heat to low; cover and simmer 1 hour.

3. Add potatoes, carrots and onions; cover and cook 20 to 25 minutes or until vegetables are tender and meat is no longer pink. Remove meat and vegetables from skillet using slotted spoon; cover and set aside. Discard orange peel and bay leaf.

4. Stir cornstarch mixture into sauce in skillet. Increase heat to medium; cook and stir until sauce is slightly thickened. Return meat and vegetables to sauce; heat through.   *Makes 6 servings*

Nutrients per Serving (1⅓ cups): Sodium: 304mg, Calories: 313, Calories from Fat: 17%, Total Fat: 6g, Saturated Fat: 1g, Cholesterol: 55mg, Carbohydrate: 31g, Fiber: 3g, Protein: 26g

Cashew Chicken

Cashew Chicken

10 ounces boneless skinless chicken breasts, diced
1 tablespoon cornstarch
1 tablespoon dry white wine
1 tablespoon reduced-sodium soy sauce
½ teaspoon garlic powder
1 teaspoon vegetable oil
6 green onions, cut into 1-inch pieces
2 cups sliced fresh mushrooms
1 red or green bell pepper, cut into strips
1 can (6 ounces) sliced water chestnuts, rinsed and drained
2 tablespoons hoisin sauce (optional)
2 cups hot cooked white rice
¼ cup cashews, toasted*

To toast cashews, spread in single layer in heavy skillet. Cook over medium heat 1 to 2 minutes or until nuts are lightly browned, stirring frequently.

1. Place chicken in large resealable food storage bag. Whisk cornstarch, wine, soy sauce and garlic powder in small bowl until smooth. Pour over chicken pieces. Seal bag; turn to coat. Marinate refrigerator 1 hour. Drain chicken; discard marinade.

2. Heat oil in wok or large nonstick skillet over medium-high heat. Add green onions; stir-fry 1 minute. Add chicken; stir-fry 2 minutes or until browned. Add mushrooms, bell pepper and water chestnuts; stir-fry 3 minutes or until vegetables are crisp-tender and chicken is cooked through. Stir in hoisin sauce, if desired; cook and stir 1 minute or until heated through.

3. Serve chicken and vegetables over rice. Top with cashews.

Makes 4 servings

Nutrients per Serving (1 cup stir-fry, ½ cup rice and 1 tablespoon cashews): Sodium: 83mg, Calories: 274, Calories from Fat: 23%, Total Fat: 7g, Saturated Fat: 1g, Cholesterol: 36mg, Carbohydrate: 34g, Fiber: 3g, Protein: 18g

Pesto Meatballs with Spaghetti

Pesto Meatballs with Spaghetti

1 pound 93% lean ground turkey
⅓ cup plain dry bread crumbs
¼ cup (1 ounce) grated Parmesan cheese
¼ cup low-fat (1%) milk
2 teaspoons dried basil
½ teaspoon garlic powder
½ teaspoon black pepper
1 tablespoon olive oil
1 can (about 14 ounces) reduced-sodium stewed tomatoes
1½ cups chopped mushrooms
1 medium green bell pepper, chopped
½ cup chopped onions
6 cups hot cooked spaghetti

1. Combine turkey, bread crumbs, cheese, milk, basil, garlic powder and black pepper in large bowl; mix well. Shape into 24 meatballs.

2. Heat oil in nonstick skillet over medium-high heat. Brown meatballs in two batches; remove from skillet. Add tomatoes, mushrooms, bell pepper and onion to skillet; simmer 5 to 6 minutes or until softened. Return meatballs to skillet; cook 10 to 15 minutes or until cooked through (165°F).

3. Serve meatballs and sauce over spaghetti.   *Makes 6 servings*

Nutrients per Serving (4 meatballs, ½ cup sauce and 1 cup spaghetti): Sodium: 164mg, Calories: 395, Calories from Fat: 23%, Total Fat: 10g, Saturated Fat: 3g, Cholesterol: 50mg, Carbohydrate: 50g, Fiber: 4g, Protein: 26g

Beef Burgers with Corn Salsa

Beef Burgers with Corn Salsa

½ cup frozen corn
½ cup chopped seeded tomato
1 can (about 4 ounces) diced green chiles, divided
1 tablespoon chopped fresh cilantro
1 tablespoon white vinegar
1 teaspoon olive oil
¼ cup fine dry bread crumbs
3 tablespoons fat-free (skim) milk
¼ teaspoon garlic powder
12 ounces 95% lean ground beef
     Lettuce leaves

1. Prepare corn according to package directions; drain. Combine corn, tomato, 2 tablespoons chiles, cilantro, vinegar and oil in small bowl. Cover and refrigerate until ready to serve.

2. Preheat broiler. Combine bread crumbs, remaining chiles, milk and garlic powder in medium bowl. Add beef; mix lightly. Shape into four ¾-inch-thick patties. Place on broiler pan.

3. Broil patties 4 inches from heat 6 to 8 minutes. Turn and broil 6 to 8 minutes or until cooked through (160°F). Serve on lettuce leaves; spoon salsa over burgers.   *Makes 4 servings*

Nutrients per Serving (1 burger with 1 tablespoon plus 2 teaspoons salsa): Sodium: 101mg, Calories: 180, Calories from Fat: 23%, Total Fat: 6g, Saturated Fat: 2g, Cholesterol: 33mg, Carbohydrate: 13g, Fiber: 2g, Protein: 19g

Bacon and Cheese Stuffed Chicken with Brown Rice

Bacon and Cheese Stuffed Chicken with Brown Rice

4 boneless skinless chicken breasts (about 4 ounces each)
½ cup (2 ounces) shredded reduced-fat Swiss cheese
2 tablespoons bacon bits
2 teaspoons paprika, divided
¼ teaspoon red pepper flakes, divided
2 teaspoons canola oil
⅔ cup uncooked quick-cooking brown rice
1¼ cups reduced-sodium chicken broth
½ cup sliced green onion

1. Cut a slit in thickest part of each chicken breast forming a pocket. Flatten chicken to ½-inch thickness. Combine cheese and bacon bits; stuff into pockets, pressing edges of chicken closed over filling. Secure with toothpicks, if desired. Sprinkle with 1 teaspoon paprika and ⅛ teaspoon red pepper.

2. Heat oil in large nonstick skillet over medium heat. Add chicken; cook 5 minutes per side or until chicken is cooked through (160°F).

3. Meanwhile, combine rice, broth, remaining 1 teaspoon paprika and ⅛ teaspoon red pepper in medium saucepan. Bring to a boil over high heat. Reduce heat; cover and simmer 10 minutes or until liquid is absorbed. Stir green onions into rice; serve with chicken.

Makes 4 servings

Nutrients per Serving (1 stuffed chicken breast with ½ cup rice): Sodium: 228mg, Calories: 284, Calories from Fat: 19%, Total Fat: 6g, Saturated Fat: 1g, Cholesterol: 76mg, Carbohydrate: 19g, Fiber: 2g, Protein: 35g

Linguine with Clams and Marinara Sauce

1⅓ cups Marinara Sauce (page 61)
1 teaspoon olive oil
¼ cup chopped shallots
3 cloves garlic, finely chopped
2 cans (6 ounces each) minced clams
2 tablespoons prepared pesto
¼ teaspoon red pepper flakes
8 ounces uncooked linguine
¼ cup chopped fresh parsley

1. Prepare Marinara Sauce.

2. Heat oil in large nonstick saucepan over medium heat. Add shallots and garlic. Cover and cook 2 minutes.

3. Drain clams; reserve ½ cup juice. Add clams, reserved juice, Marinara Sauce, pesto and red pepper to saucepan. Cook 10 minutes, stirring occasionally.

4. Cook linguine according to package directions, omitting salt. Drain. Spoon sauce evenly over linguine; top with parsley.

Makes 4 servings

Nutrients per Serving (¼ of total recipe): Sodium: 293mg, Calories: 398, Calories from Fat: 14%, Total Fat: 6g, Saturated Fat: 1g, Cholesterol: 58mg, Carbohydrate: 54g, Fiber: 4g, Protein: 32g

Marinara Sauce

1½ tablespoons olive oil
3 cloves garlic, minced
1 can (28 ounces) Italian plum tomatoes, drained, juice reserved and chopped
¼ cup tomato paste
2 teaspoons dried basil
½ teaspoon sugar
¼ teaspoon salt
¼ teaspoon red pepper flakes

Heat oil in large skillet over medium heat. Add garlic; cook and stir 3 minutes. Stir in remaining ingredients. Bring to a boil. Reduce heat to low; simmer 10 minutes. *Makes about 3½ cups*

Swiss, Tomato and Turkey Patty Melt

1 pound ground turkey
½ (0.4-ounce) packet ranch salad dressing mix
1 medium green onion, finely chopped
1 teaspoon olive oil
2 slices reduced-fat Swiss cheese, halved diagonally
1 medium tomato, diced

1. Combine turkey, salad dressing mix and green onion in medium bowl; mix well. Shape into four patties.

2. Heat oil in large nonstick skillet over medium heat; tilt skillet to coat bottom evenly. Add patties; cook 14 minutes or until cooked through (165°F), turning once.

3. Remove skillet from heat. Top each patty with cheese. Cover and let stand 2 to 3 minutes or until cheese is melted. Top each patty with diced tomato. *Makes 4 servings*

Nutrients per Serving (1 patty): Sodium: 253mg, Calories: 239, Calories from Fat: 41%, Total Fat: 11g, Saturated Fat: 3g, Cholesterol: 75mg, Carbohydrate: 3g, Fiber: <1g, Protein: 28g

Pork Tenderloin with Sherry-Mushroom Sauce

Pork Tenderloin with Sherry-Mushroom Sauce

1 to 2 pork tenderloins (about 1 to 1½ pounds total)
1 tablespoon reduced-fat margarine
1½ cups chopped button mushrooms or shiitake
    mushroom caps
2 tablespoons sliced green onion
1 clove garlic, minced
⅓ cup water
1 tablespoon cornstarch
1 tablespoon chopped fresh parsley
1 tablespoon dry sherry
½ teaspoon beef bouillon granules
½ teaspoon dried thyme leaves
    Dash black pepper

1. Preheat oven to 375°F. Place pork on rack in shallow roasting pan. Insert meat thermometer into thickest part of tenderloin. Roast, uncovered, 25 to 35 minutes or until thermometer registers 160°F. Tent with foil; let stand 5 to 10 minutes.

2. Melt margarine in small saucepan over medium heat. Add mushrooms, green onion and garlic; cook and stir until vegetables are tender. Stir in remaining ingredients. Bring to a boil; cook and stir 2 to 3 minutes or until thickened. Cook and stir 2 minutes more. Slice pork; serve with sauce. _Makes 4 servings_

Nutrients per Serving (¼ of total recipe): Sodium: 205mg, Calories: 179, Calories from Fat: 30%, Total Fat: 6g, Saturated Fat: 2g, Cholesterol: 81mg, Carbohydrate: 4g, Fiber: <1g, Protein: 26g

Shrimp and Chicken Paella

Shrimp and Chicken Paella

¾ cup cooked rice

2 cans (about 14 ounces each) no-salt-added diced tomatoes

½ teaspoon ground turmeric *or* ⅛ teaspoon saffron threads

1 package (¾ pound) medium shrimp, peeled and deveined (about 3 cups)

2 chicken tenders (about 4 ounces), cut into 1-inch pieces

1 cup frozen peas

1. Preheat oven to 400°F. Spray 8-inch glass baking dish with nonstick cooking spray. Spread rice in dish.

2. Pour one can of tomatoes with juice over rice; sprinkle turmeric over tomatoes. Arrange shrimp and chicken over tomatoes. Top with peas.

3. Drain remaining can of tomatoes, discarding juice. Spread tomatoes evenly over shrimp and chicken. Cover; bake 30 minutes. Let stand, covered, 5 minutes before serving. To serve, spoon into shallow bowls.   *Makes 4 servings*

Nutrients per Serving (1 cup): Sodium: 152mg, Calories: 175, Calories from Fat: 5%, Total Fat: 1g, Saturated Fat: <1g, Cholesterol: 97mg, Carbohydrate: 19g, Fiber: 2g, Protein: 19g

Italian-Style Meat Loaf

Italian-Style Meat Loaf

1 can (6 ounces) no-salt-added tomato paste
½ cup water
½ cup dry red wine
1 teaspoon minced garlic
½ teaspoon dried basil
½ teaspoon dried oregano
¼ teaspoon salt
¾ pound 95% lean ground beef
¾ pound 93% lean ground turkey breast
1 cup fresh whole wheat bread crumbs (2 slices whole wheat bread)
½ cup shredded zucchini
¼ cup cholesterol-free egg substitute *or* 2 egg whites

1. Preheat oven to 350°F. Combine tomato paste, water, wine, garlic, basil, oregano and salt in small saucepan. Bring to a boil; reduce heat to low. Simmer, uncovered, 15 minutes.

2. Combine beef, turkey, bread crumbs, zucchini, egg substitute and ½ cup tomato mixture in large bowl; mix lightly. Shape into loaf; place in ungreased 9×5-inch loaf pan.

3. Bake 45 minutes. Drain fat. Spread remaining tomato mixture over meat loaf. Bake 15 minutes or until cooked through (165°F). Let stand 10 minutes before slicing.   *Makes 8 servings*

Nutrients per Serving (1 slice): Sodium: 212mg, Calories: 187, Calories from Fat: 29%, Total Fat: 6g, Saturated Fat: 2g, Cholesterol: 56mg, Carbohydrate: 12g, Fiber: 2g, Protein: 19g

Macaroni and Cheese with Mixed Vegetables

Macaroni and Cheese with Mixed Vegetables

1¼ cups fat-free (skim) milk, divided
2 tablespoons all-purpose flour
½ cup (2 ounces) shredded reduced-fat sharp Cheddar cheese
½ cup (2 ounces) shredded Parmesan cheese
1½ cups frozen mixed vegetables, cooked and drained
1⅓ cups cooked whole wheat elbow macaroni, rotini or penne
¼ teaspoon salt (optional)
⅛ teaspoon black pepper

1. Preheat oven to 325°F. Spray 1½-quart baking dish with nonstick cooking spray.

2. Whisk ¼ cup milk and flour in medium saucepan until smooth. Add remaining 1 cup milk; stir until well blended. Cook over medium heat until thickened, stirring constantly.

3. Combine cheeses in separate medium bowl. Stir half of cheese mixture into saucepan. Add vegetables, macaroni, salt, if desired, and pepper.

4. Spoon macaroni mixture into prepared baking dish. Sprinkle with remaining cheese mixture. Bake 20 minutes or until cheese is melted and macaroni is heated through. Let stand 5 minutes before serving. *Makes 4 servings*

Nutrients per Serving (¾ cup): Sodium: 330mg, Calories: 240, Calories from Fat: 23%, Total Fat: 6g, Saturated Fat: 4g, Cholesterol: 20mg, Carbohydrate: 32g, Fiber: 5g, Protein: 15g

Roast Turkey Breast with Spinach-Blue Cheese Stuffing

Roast Turkey Breast with Spinach-Blue Cheese Stuffing

1 frozen whole boneless turkey breast, thawed
  (about 3½ to 4 pounds)
1 package (10 ounces) frozen chopped spinach, thawed
  and squeezed dry
2 ounces blue cheese or feta cheese
2 ounces reduced-fat cream cheese
½ cup finely chopped green onions
1½ tablespoons Dijon mustard
1½ tablespoons dried basil
2 teaspoons dried oregano
  Black pepper and paprika

1. Preheat oven to 350°F. Spray shallow roasting pan and rack with nonstick cooking spray.

2. Unroll turkey breast; rinse and pat dry. Place turkey between sheets of plastic wrap or waxed paper. Pound turkey to 1-inch thickness using flat side of meat mallet or rolling pin. Remove and discard skin from one side of turkey breast; place turkey skin side down on work surface.

3. Combine spinach, blue cheese, cream cheese, green onions, mustard, basil and oregano in medium bowl; mix well. Spread evenly over turkey breast. Roll up turkey so skin is on top. Tie closed with kitchen string.

4. Place turkey breast on prepared rack; sprinkle with pepper and paprika. Roast 1½ hours or until no longer pink in center. Let stand 10 minutes before removing skin and slicing.   *Makes 14 servings*

Nutrients per Serving (1 slice): Sodium: 144mg, Calories: 135, Calories from Fat: 27%, Total Fat: 4g, Saturated Fat: 2g, Cholesterol: 50mg, Carbohydrate: 2g, Fiber: 1g, Protein: 22g

Beef & Artichoke Casserole

Beef & Artichoke Casserole

¾ pound 95% lean ground beef
½ cup sliced mushrooms
¼ cup chopped onion
1 clove garlic, minced
1 can (14 ounces) artichoke hearts, drained and chopped
½ cup dry bread crumbs
¼ cup grated Parmesan cheese
1 tablespoon chopped fresh rosemary leaves *or* 1 teaspoon
    dried rosemary
1½ teaspoons chopped fresh marjoram *or* ½ teaspoon
    dried marjoram
Salt and black pepper
3 egg whites

1. Preheat oven to 400°F. Spray 1-quart casserole with nonstick cooking spray.

2. Brown beef in medium skillet over medium-high heat 6 to 8 minutes, stirring to break up meat. Drain fat. Add mushrooms, onion and garlic; cook and stir 5 minutes or until tender.

3. Combine beef mixture, artichokes, bread crumbs, cheese, rosemary and marjoram; mix lightly. Season with salt and pepper.

4. Beat egg whites in medium bowl with electric mixer at high speed until stiff peaks form; fold into beef mixture. Spoon into prepared casserole.

5. Bake 20 minutes or until edges are lightly browned.

Makes 4 servings

Nutrients per Serving (¼ of total recipe): Sodium: 330mg, Calories: 260, Calories from Fat: 24%, Total Fat: 7g, Saturated Fat: 3g, Cholesterol: 55mg, Carbohydrate: 24g, Fiber: 9g, Protein: 28g

Three-Cheese Manicotti

Nonstick cooking spray
1 cup sliced cremini mushrooms
2 cups reduced-sodium meatless pasta sauce
1 cup fat-free ricotta cheese
¼ cup grated Parmesan cheese
¼ cup cholesterol-free egg substitute
1 tablespoon chopped fresh basil
⅛ teaspoon salt
¼ teaspoon black pepper
6 cooked manicotti shells
¼ cup (1 ounce) shredded reduced-fat mozzarella cheese

1. Preheat oven to 350°F. Spray large skillet with cooking spray. Add mushrooms; cook over medium heat 5 minutes or until tender. Stir in pasta sauce. Spread ½ cup sauce mixture in bottom of 11×7-inch glass baking dish.

2. Combine ricotta cheese, Parmesan cheese, egg substitute, basil, salt and pepper in medium bowl; mix well. Spoon about ¼ cup mixture evenly into each manicotti shell. Place manicotti in baking dish (they should fit snugly). Top with remaining pasta sauce. Cover dish loosely with foil.

3. Bake 28 to 30 minutes or until sauce is bubbly. Uncover; sprinkle with mozzarella cheese. Bake 5 to 10 minutes or until cheese is melted. Let stand 5 minutes. *Makes 6 servings*

Nutrients per Serving (⅙ of total recipe): Sodium: 263mg, Calories: 193, Calories from Fat: 28%, Total Fat: 6g, Saturated Fat: 2g, Cholesterol: 15mg, Carbohydrate: 23g, Fiber: 3g, Protein: 11g

Fajita Pile-Ups

2 teaspoons vegetable oil, divided

¾ pound beef top sirloin steak, trimmed of fat, cut into thin strips

2 teaspoons salt-free steak seasoning

½ medium lime

1 medium green bell pepper, cut into ½-inch strips

1 medium red or yellow bell pepper, cut into ½-inch strips

1 large onion, cut into ½-inch wedges

1 cup cherry tomatoes, halved

½ teaspoon ground cumin

4 (6-inch) corn tortillas

½ cup fat-free sour cream

2 tablespoons chopped fresh cilantro (optional)

Lime wedges (optional)

1. Heat 1 teaspoon oil in large nonstick skillet over medium-high heat. Add steak; sprinkle with seasoning. Cook and stir 3 minutes or just until slightly pink in center. *Do not overcook.* Transfer to plate. Squeeze lime half over steak. Cover to keep warm.

2. Add remaining 1 teaspoon oil to skillet. Add bell peppers and onion; cook and stir 8 minutes or just until tender. Add tomatoes; cook and stir 1 minute. Add steak with any accumulated juices and cumin to skillet; cook and stir 1 minute.

3. Warm tortillas according to package directions. Top tortillas evenly with steak mixture. Serve with sour cream. Garnish with cilantro and lime wedges. *Makes 4 servings*

Nutrients per Serving (1 tortilla with 1¼ cups steak mixture): Sodium: 90mg, Calories: 252, Calories from Fat: 25%, Total Fat: 7g, Saturated Fat: 2g, Cholesterol: 41mg, Carbohydrate: 24g, Fiber: 4g, Protein: 24g

Side Dishes

Confetti Black Beans

1 cup dried black beans
3 cups water
1 can (about 14 ounces) reduced-sodium chicken or
    vegetable broth
1 bay leaf
1½ teaspoons olive oil
1 medium onion, chopped
¼ cup chopped red bell pepper
¼ cup chopped yellow bell pepper
2 cloves garlic, minced
1 jalapeño pepper,* finely chopped
1 large tomato, seeded and chopped
½ teaspoon salt
⅛ teaspoon black pepper
    Hot pepper sauce (optional)

Jalapeño peppers can sting and irritate the skin, so wear rubber gloves when handling peppers and do not touch your eyes.

1. Sort and rinse beans; cover with water. Soak 8 hours or overnight. Drain.

2. Place beans and broth in large saucepan; bring to a boil over high heat. Add bay leaf. Reduce heat to low; cover and simmer 1½ hours or until beans are tender.

3. Heat oil in large skillet over medium heat. Add onion, bell peppers, garlic and jalapeño; cook and stir 8 to 10 minutes or until onion is translucent. Add tomato, salt and black pepper; cook 5 minutes.

4. Add onion mixture to beans; cook 15 to 20 minutes. Remove bay leaf before serving. Serve with hot sauce, if desired.

Makes 6 servings

Nutrients per Serving (½ cup): Sodium: 209mg, Calories: 146, Calories from Fat: 12%, Total Fat: 2g, Saturated Fat: <1g, Cholesterol: 0mg, Carbohydrate: 24g, Fiber: 6g, Protein: 8g

Sweet Potato Fries

Sweet Potato Fries

  1 large sweet potato (about 8 ounces)
  2 teaspoons olive oil
  ¼ teaspoon kosher salt
  ¼ teaspoon black pepper
  ¼ teaspoon ground red pepper
    Honey or maple syrup (optional)

1. Preheat oven to 350°F. Spray baking sheet with nonstick cooking spray.

2. Peel sweet potato; cut lengthwise into long thin spears. Toss with oil, salt, black pepper and red pepper on prepared baking sheet. Arrange potatoes in single layer (potatoes should not touch).

3. Bake 45 minutes or until lightly browned. Serve with honey for dipping, if desired. *Makes 2 servings*

Nutrients per Serving (½ of total recipe): Sodium: 301mg, Calories: 139, Calories from Fat: 32%, Total Fat: 5g, Saturated Fat: <1g, Cholesterol: 0mg, Carbohydrate: 23g, Fiber: 4g, Protein: 2g

Beets in Spicy Mustard Sauce

Beets in Spicy Mustard Sauce

3 pounds beets, trimmed
¼ cup reduced-fat sour cream
2 tablespoons spicy brown mustard
2 teaspoons lemon juice
2 cloves garlic, minced
¼ teaspoon black pepper
⅛ teaspoon dried thyme

1. Place beets in large saucepan; add enough water to cover by 1 inch. Bring to a boil over medium-high heat. Reduce heat to medium-low; cover and simmer 25 minutes or until tender. Drain well. Peel beets; cut into ¼-inch-thick slices.

2. Combine sour cream, mustard, lemon juice, garlic, pepper and thyme in small saucepan; cook and stir over medium heat until heated through. Spoon sauce over beets; toss gently to coat.

Makes 4 servings

Nutrients per Serving (¼ of total recipe): Sodium: 253mg, Calories: 116, Calories from Fat: 16%, Total Fat: 2g, Saturated Fat: <1g, Cholesterol: 6mg, Carbohydrate: 21g, Fiber: 6g, Protein: 4g

Savory Bread Stuffing

Savory Bread Stuffing

2 teaspoons canola oil
½ cup chopped onion
½ cup chopped celery
1 cup fat-free reduced-sodium chicken broth
½ cup unsweetened apple juice
4 cups (7 ounces) seasoned cubed bread stuffing mix
¾ cup diced unpeeled red apple
¼ cup chopped pecans, toasted*

*To toast pecans, spread in single layer on baking sheet. Bake in preheated 350°F oven 8 to 10 minutes or until golden brown, stirring frequently. Cool before using.

1. Preheat oven to 350°F. Spray 2-quart casserole with nonstick cooking spray.

2. Heat oil in medium saucepan over medium heat. Add onion and celery; cook and stir 7 to 8 minutes or until vegetables are tender and lightly browned on edges. Stir in broth and juice; bring to a boil over high heat. Remove from heat; stir in stuffing mix, apple and pecans; mix well. Transfer to prepared casserole.

3. Cover and bake 30 to 35 minutes or until heated through.

Makes 12 servings

Variations: If your diet plan permits, stir in 2 tablespoons light butter with canola oil before serving. Sprinkle with additional pecans.

Nutrients per Serving (½ cup): Sodium: 317mg, Calories: 111, Calories from Fat: 24%, Total Fat: 3g, Saturated Fat: <1g, Cholesterol: 0mg, Carbohydrate: 18g, Fiber: 2g, Protein: 3g

Wild Rice, Mushroom and Spinach Skillet

Wild Rice, Mushroom and Spinach Skillet

⅓ cup uncooked wild rice
⅓ cup uncooked brown rice
⅓ cup uncooked long grain white rice
1½ cups water
1 can (10 ounces) condensed reduced-sodium chicken broth, undiluted
2 tablespoons margarine
2 cups sliced shiitake mushrooms
2 cups quartered cremini (brown) mushrooms
2 cups sliced bok choy
2 cups shredded spinach leaves
¼ cup (1 ounce) crumbled feta cheese

1. Combine wild rice, brown rice, white rice, water and broth in medium saucepan. Bring to a boil over high heat. Reduce heat to low; cover and simmer 45 minutes or until rice is tender.

2. Melt margarine in large saucepan over medium heat. Add mushrooms; cook and stir 3 minutes. Add bok choy and spinach; cook and stir 3 minutes or until greens are wilted.

3. Stir in rice. Gently stir in cheese just before serving.

Makes 10 servings

Nutrients per Serving (⅒ of total recipe): Sodium: 117mg, Calories: 130, Calories from Fat: 28%, Total Fat: 4g, Saturated Fat: 2g, Cholesterol: 6mg, Carbohydrate: 19g, Fiber: 2g, Protein: 4g

Skillet Succotash

Skillet Succotash

1 teaspoon canola oil
½ cup diced onion
½ cup diced green bell pepper
½ cup diced celery
½ teaspoon paprika
¾ cup frozen white or yellow corn
¾ cup frozen lima beans
½ cup canned low-sodium diced tomatoes
1 teaspoon dried parsley flakes *or* 1 tablespoon
   minced fresh parsley
¼ teaspoon salt
¼ teaspoon black pepper

1. Heat oil in large skillet over medium heat. Add onion, bell pepper and celery; cook and stir 5 minutes or until onion is translucent and pepper and celery are crisp-tender. Stir in paprika.

2. Add corn, lima beans and tomatoes. Reduce heat; cover and simmer 20 minutes or until beans are tender. Stir in parsley, salt and black pepper just before serving. *Makes 4 servings*

Tip: For additional flavor, add 1 clove minced garlic and 1 bay leaf to skillet with corn, lima beans and tomatoes. Remove and discard bay leaf before serving.

Nutrients per Serving (½ cup): Sodium: 187mg, Calories: 99, Calories from Fat: 18%, Total Fat: 2g, Saturated Fat: <1g, Cholesterol: 0mg, Carbohydrate: 19g, Fiber: 4g, Protein: 4g

Hot and Spicy Spuds

Hot and Spicy Spuds

4 medium baking potatoes
Nonstick cooking spray
1 cup chopped onion
½ cup chopped green bell pepper
2 cloves garlic, minced
1 teaspoon olive oil
1 can (about 15 ounces) reduced-sodium kidney beans,
    rinsed and drained
1 can (about 14 ounces) no-salt-added diced tomatoes
1 can (4 ounces) diced mild green chiles
¼ cup chopped fresh cilantro or parsley
1 teaspoon ground cumin
1 teaspoon chili powder
¼ teaspoon ground red pepper
¼ cup reduced-fat sour cream
¼ cup (1 ounce) shredded reduced-fat Cheddar cheese

1. Preheat oven to 350°F. Scrub potatoes; pierce with fork. Bake 1¼ to 1½ hours or until tender.

2. Meanwhile, spray large saucepan with cooking spray; heat over medium heat. Add onion, bell pepper, garlic and oil; cook and stir until vegetables are tender.

3. Stir in beans, tomatoes with juice, chiles, cilantro, cumin, chili powder and red pepper. Bring to a boil over high heat. Reduce heat to medium-low. Cover and simmer 8 minutes, stirring occasionally.

4. Gently roll potatoes to loosen pulp. Cut lengthwise slit in each potato. Place on four plates. Press ends to open slits. Spoon bean mixture over potatoes. Top with sour cream and cheese.

Makes 4 servings

Nutrients per Serving (¼ of total recipe): Sodium: 88mg, Calories: 384, Calories from Fat: 12%, Total Fat: 5g, Saturated Fat: 1g, Cholesterol: 11mg, Carbohydrate: 72g, Fiber: 8g, Protein: 15g

French Carrot Medley

French Carrot Medley

2 cups fresh or frozen sliced carrots
¾ cup fresh squeezed orange juice
1 can (4 ounces) sliced mushrooms, undrained
4 stalks celery, sliced
2 tablespoons chopped onion
½ teaspoon dried dill weed
2 teaspoons cornstarch
¼ cup cold water
Salt and black pepper (optional)

1. Combine carrots, orange juice, mushrooms, celery, onion and dill in medium saucepan. Cover and simmer 12 to 15 minutes or until carrots are tender.

2. Stir cornstarch into water in small bowl until smooth. Stir into vegetable mixture; cook and stir until mixture is thickened and bubbly. Season with salt and pepper, if desired.

Makes 6 servings

Nutrients per Serving (⅙ of total recipe): Sodium: 118mg, Calories: 42, Calories from Fat: 0%, Total Fat: <1g, Saturated Fat: <1g, Cholesterol: 0mg, Carbohydrate: 10g, Fiber: 2g, Protein: 1g

Spinach Parmesan Risotto

Spinach Parmesan Risotto

3⅔ cups reduced-sodium chicken or vegetable broth
½ teaspoon white pepper
   Nonstick cooking spray
1 cup uncooked arborio rice
1½ cups chopped fresh spinach
½ cup fresh or frozen peas
1 tablespoon minced fresh dill *or* 1 teaspoon dried dill weed
½ cup grated Parmesan cheese
1 teaspoon grated lemon peel

1. Combine broth and white pepper in medium saucepan; bring to a boil over medium-high heat. Reduce heat; keep broth at a simmer.

2. Spray large saucepan with cooking spray; heat over medium-low heat. Add rice; cook and stir 1 minute. Stir ⅔ cup hot broth into saucepan; cook until broth is absorbed, stirring constantly.

3. Stir in remaining hot broth, ½ cup at a time, stirring frequently until broth is absorbed before adding next ½ cup. When last ½ cup of broth is added, stir in spinach, peas and dill. Cook, stirring gently, until all broth is absorbed and rice is just tender but still firm. (Total cooking time is about 20 minutes.)

4. Remove saucepan from heat; stir in cheese and lemon peel.

Makes 6 servings

Note: Arborio rice, an Italian short-grain rice, has large, plump grains with a delicious nutty taste. It is traditionally used for risotto dishes because its high starch content produces a creamy texture.

Nutrients per Serving (½ cup): Sodium: 198mg, Calories: 179, Calories from Fat: 15%, Total Fat: 3g, Saturated Fat: 2g, Cholesterol: 7mg, Carbohydrate: 30g, Fiber: 1g, Protein: 7g

Brussels Sprouts with Bacon, Thyme and Raisins

Brussels Sprouts with Bacon, Thyme and Raisins

1 pound brussels sprouts, trimmed and cut in half
½ cup reduced-sodium chicken broth
⅓ cup golden raisins
1 thick slice applewood smoked bacon, chopped
1 tablespoon chopped fresh thyme

1. Combine brussels sprouts and broth in large skillet. Cover and bring to a boil over high heat. Reduce heat; simmer 5 minutes.

2. Add raisins; cook and stir 4 to 5 minutes or until broth is absorbed. Add bacon; cook and stir 3 to 4 minutes or until brussels sprouts are tender. Stir in thyme.   *Makes 4 servings*

Nutrients per Serving (¾ cup): Sodium: 110mg, Calories: 109, Calories from Fat: 17%, Total Fat: 2g, Saturated Fat: <1g, Cholesterol: 3mg, Carbohydrate: 21g, Fiber: 5g, Protein: 6g

Green Beans with Maple-Bacon Dressing

½ cup fat-free low-sodium chicken broth or water
1 package (16 ounces) frozen French-style green beans
1 tablespoon bacon bits
1 tablespoon maple syrup
1 tablespoon cider vinegar
¼ teaspoon black pepper

1. Bring broth to a boil in large saucepan over medium heat. Add green beans; cover and simmer 7 minutes or until green beans are crisp-tender. Drain; place green beans in large bowl.

2. Combine bacon bits, maple syrup, vinegar and pepper in small bowl. Pour over green beans; toss to coat.   *Makes 6 servings*

Nutrients per Serving (½ cup): Sodium: 324mg, Calories: 76, Calories from Fat: 47%, Total Fat: 4g, Saturated Fat: 1g, Cholesterol: 8mg, Carbohydrate: 7g, Fiber: 5g, Protein: 3g

Desserts

Pineapple-Raisin Cake

2 eggs
1 cup thawed frozen unsweetened pineapple juice concentrate
¼ cup (½ stick) butter, melted
1 teaspoon vanilla
1⅓ cups all-purpose flour
⅔ cup old-fashioned oats
1 teaspoon baking soda
1 teaspoon ground cinnamon
½ teaspoon ground ginger
¼ teaspoon salt
⅛ teaspoon ground nutmeg
1 can (8 ounces) crushed pineapple in unsweetened juice,
   well drained
¾ cup lightly toasted chopped pecans
½ cup golden raisins

1. Preheat oven to 350°F. Spray 12×8-inch baking dish with nonstick cooking spray.

2. Beat eggs in large bowl. Stir in pineapple juice concentrate, butter and vanilla. Add flour, oats, baking soda, cinnamon, ginger, salt and nutmeg; mix well. Stir in pineapple, pecans and raisins. Pour into prepared baking dish.

3. Bake 18 to 20 minutes or until firm. Cool completely on wire rack; cut into bars. Store in airtight container.   *Makes 16 bars*

Nutrients per Serving (1 bar): Sodium: 156mg, Calories: 181, Calories from Fat: 40%, Total Fat: 8g, Saturated Fat: 2g, Cholesterol: 35mg, Carbohydrate: 26g, Fiber: 2g, Protein: 3g

Cheesy Cherry Turnovers

Cheesy Cherry Turnovers

   Butter-flavored cooking spray
   1 package (8 ounces) reduced-fat cream cheese, softened
   1 cup low-fat (1%) cottage cheese
   ½ cup sugar, divided
   1 teaspoon vanilla
   1 can (16½ ounces) dark sweet pitted cherries, rinsed and drained
   8 sheets frozen phyllo dough, thawed
   1 cup whole wheat bread crumbs
   1 teaspoon ground cinnamon

1. Preheat oven to 350°F. Spray baking sheet with cooking spray.

2. Beat cream cheese, cottage cheese, ¼ cup sugar and vanilla in medium bowl with electric mixer at medium speed until well blended. Stir in cherries.

3. Spray one sheet of phyllo dough with cooking spray; fold sheet lengthwise in half to form rectangle. Sprinkle with 2 tablespoons bread crumbs. Place ⅓ cup of cheese mixture on upper left corner of sheet. Fold right corner over mixture to form triangle. Continue folding turnover like a flag, making triangular packet. Repeat with remaining ingredients. Place turnovers on prepared baking sheet.

4. Combine remaining ¼ cup sugar with cinnamon. Sprinkle over turnovers.

5. Bake 12 to 15 minutes or until turnovers are crisp and golden brown. Serve warm or cold.   *Makes 8 servings*

Nutrients per Serving (1 turnover): Sodium: 314mg, Calories: 170, Calories from Fat: 32%, Total Fat: 6g, Saturated Fat: 3g, Cholesterol: 11mg, Carbohydrate: 24g, Fiber: 1g, Protein: 8g

Mango-Citrus Pudding Cake

Mango-Citrus Pudding Cake

1½ cups peeled, seeded and chopped mango *or* 1 can
    (11 ounces) mandarin orange sections, drained
½ cup sugar
¼ cup all-purpose flour
1 tablespoon grated orange peel
¼ teaspoon ground nutmeg
⅛ teaspoon salt
2 tablespoons lemon juice
1 tablespoon butter or margarine, melted
3 egg yolks, beaten
2 containers (6 ounces each) orange or lemon
    reduced-fat yogurt
⅓ cup fat-free (skim) milk
3 egg whites
    Fresh mint leaves (optional)

1. Preheat oven to 350°F. Spray 8-inch square baking dish with nonstick cooking spray. Arrange mango pieces in bottom of dish.

2. Combine sugar, flour, orange peel, nutmeg and salt in medium bowl. Stir in lemon juice and butter. Add egg yolks, yogurt and milk; mix well.

3. Beat egg whites in large bowl with electric mixer at high speed until stiff peaks form. Gently fold egg whites into yogurt mixture until blended. Spoon over mango in baking dish.

4. Place dish in larger baking pan. Pour hot water into pan around baking dish to depth of 1 inch.

5. Bake 40 minutes or until top is golden brown. Remove baking dish from larger pan; cool on wire rack 20 minutes. Spoon into dessert dishes. Garnish with mint, if desired. *Makes 9 servings*

Nutrients per Serving (⅑ of total recipe): Sodium: 89mg, Calories: 147, Calories from Fat: 24%, Total Fat: 4g, Saturated Fat: 2g, Cholesterol: 75mg, Carbohydrate: 25g, Fiber: 1g, Protein: 5g

Date Gingerbread

Date Gingerbread

1¼ cups plus 1 teaspoon all-purpose flour, divided
¾ cup finely chopped pitted dates (about 18 whole dates)
½ cup whole wheat flour
¼ cup packed brown sugar
1 tablespoon (½ ounce) finely chopped candied ginger
½ teaspoon baking powder
½ teaspoon baking soda
½ teaspoon ground ginger
½ teaspoon ground nutmeg
½ cup water
½ cup molasses
¼ cup canola or vegetable oil
2 egg whites
Whipped cream (optional)

1. Preheat oven to 350°F. Spray 8-inch round cake pan with nonstick cooking spray. Dust with 1 teaspoon all-purpose flour.

2. Combine remaining 1¼ cups all-purpose flour, dates, whole wheat flour, brown sugar, candied ginger, baking powder, baking soda, ground ginger and nutmeg in large bowl. Add water, molasses, oil and egg whites; beat with electric mixer at low speed until combined. Beat at high speed 2 minutes. Pour into prepared pan.

3. Bake 38 to 40 minutes or until toothpick inserted into center comes out clean. Cool in pan 10 minutes. Cut into wedges and serve warm. Garnish with whipped cream.   *Makes 8 servings*

Nutrients per Serving (1 wedge): Sodium: 109mg, Calories: 283, Calories from Fat: 22%, Total Fat: 7g, Saturated Fat: <1g, Cholesterol: 0mg, Carbohydrate: 52g, Fiber: 3g, Protein: 4g

Shortcakes with Warm Apple-Cinnamon Topping

Shortcakes with Warm Apple-Cinnamon Topping

1 cup reduced-fat biscuit baking mix
3 teaspoons sugar, divided
1 teaspoon grated orange peel
3 to 4 tablespoons fat-free half-and-half
    Warm Apple-Cinnamon Topping (recipe follows)
3 tablespoons fat-free whipped topping

1. Preheat oven to 450°F. Line baking sheet with parchment paper.

2. Combine biscuit mix, 2 teaspoons sugar and orange peel in medium bowl. Stir in half-and-half, 1 tablespoon at a time, until soft dough forms. Gently knead ten times. Turn dough out onto work surface. Cut into 2-inch circles with biscuit cutter, reworking dough to make six shortcakes. Place on prepared baking sheet; sprinkle with remaining 1 teaspoon sugar.

3. Bake 12 to 15 minutes or until golden brown. Meanwhile, prepare Warm Apple-Cinnamon Topping.

4. Split each shortcake in half crosswise; fill with topping. Spoon 1½ teaspoons whipped topping over each shortcake. Serve immediately. *Makes 6 servings*

Nutrients per Serving (1 shortcake): Sodium: 271mg, Calories: 137, Calories from Fat: 20%, Total Fat: 3g, Saturated Fat: <1g, Cholesterol: 1mg, Carbohydrate: 28g, Fiber: 2g, Protein: 2g

Warm Apple-Cinnamon Topping

1½ teaspoons margarine
3 cups thinly sliced unpeeled apple (1 large or 2 small apples), preferably Gala, Fuji or Pink Lady
¼ teaspoon ground cinnamon
½ cup apple juice
1 teaspoon sugar

Melt margarine in large nonstick skillet. Add apple slices and cinnamon; cook over medium heat 3 to 5 minutes or until apples are tender. Add juice and sugar; cook over high heat 30 seconds or until juice is reduced by half and mixture is syrupy.

Chocolate Chip Brownies

Chocolate Chip Brownies

¾ cup granulated sugar
½ cup (1 stick) butter
2 tablespoons water
2 cups (12 ounces) semisweet chocolate chips, divided
1½ teaspoons vanilla
1¼ cups all-purpose flour
½ teaspoon baking soda
½ teaspoon salt
2 eggs
Powdered sugar (optional)

1. Preheat oven to 350°F. Grease 9-inch square baking pan.

2. Combine granulated sugar, butter and water in medium microwavable bowl. Microwave on HIGH 1½ to 2 minutes or until butter is melted. Stir in 1 cup chocolate chips; stir until chips are melted and mixture is smooth. Stir in vanilla; let stand 5 minutes to cool slightly.

3. Combine flour, baking soda and salt in small bowl. Add eggs to chocolate mixture, one at a time, beating well after each addition. Add flour mixture; mix well. Stir in remaining 1 cup chocolate chips. Pour into prepared pan.

4. Bake 25 minutes for fudgy brownies or 30 to 35 minutes for cakelike brownies. Cool completely in pan on wire rack. Cut into 2¼-inch squares. Place powdered sugar in fine-mesh strainer and sprinkle over brownies, if desired. Store tightly covered at room temperature or freeze up to 3 months. *Makes 16 brownies*

Nutrients per Serving (1 brownie): Sodium: 170mg, Calories: 230, Calories from Fat: 51%, Total Fat: 13g, Saturated Fat: 8g, Cholesterol: 40mg, Carbohydrate: 30g, Fiber: 2g, Protein: 3g

Peach-Almond Cheesecake

Peach-Almond Cheesecake

- **2 packages (8 ounces each) reduced-fat cream cheese, softened**
- **⅓ cup sugar**
- **2 eggs**
- **5 tablespoons peach or apricot fruit spread, divided**
- **¼ teaspoon almond extract**
- **1 (6-ounce) graham cracker crust**
- **½ (16-ounce) package frozen unsweetened peach slices, thawed**
- **¼ cup slivered almonds, toasted***

*To toast almonds, spread in single layer on ungreased baking sheet. Bake in preheated 350°F oven 8 to 10 minutes or until light brown, stirring occasionally.

1. Preheat oven to 325°F.

2. Beat cream cheese and sugar in large bowl with electric mixer at medium speed 1 minute or until smooth. Beat in eggs, one at a time, until well blended. Beat in 3 tablespoons fruit spread and almond extract just until blended.

3. Pour cream cheese mixture into crust. Bake about 45 minutes or until filling is set. Cool completely on wire rack. Cover and refrigerate at least 4 hours.

4. Arrange peach slices on top of cheesecake. Melt remaining 2 tablespoons fruit spread in small saucepan over low heat. Spoon over peach slices. Sprinkle with almonds. Refrigerate 30 minutes before serving. *Makes 10 servings*

Nutrients per Serving (⅒ of total recipe): Sodium: 245mg, Calories: 274, Calories from Fat: 49%, Total Fat: 15g, Saturated Fat: 6g, Cholesterol: 68mg, Carbohydrate: 29g, Fiber: 1g, Protein: 8g

Apricot Crumb Squares

Apricot Crumb Squares

1 package (about 18 ounces) light yellow cake mix
1 teaspoon ground cinnamon
½ teaspoon ground nutmeg
¼ cup plus 2 tablespoons cold margarine, cut into pieces
¾ cup uncooked multigrain oatmeal cereal or
      old-fashioned oats
1 egg
2 egg whites
1 tablespoon water
1 jar (10 ounces) apricot fruit spread
2 tablespoons packed light brown sugar

1. Preheat oven to 350°F.

2. Combine cake mix, cinnamon and nutmeg in medium bowl. Cut in margarine with pastry blender or two knives until coarse crumbs form. Stir in cereal. Reserve 1 cup crumb mixture. Add egg, egg whites and water to remaining crumb mixture; stir until well blended.

3. Spread evenly in ungreased 13×9-inch baking pan; top with fruit spread. Sprinkle reserved crumb mixture over fruit spread; sprinkle with brown sugar.

4. Bake 35 to 40 minutes or until top is golden brown. Cool in pan on wire rack; cut into 15 squares. *Makes 15 servings*

Nutrients per Serving (1 square): Sodium: 299mg, Calories: 267, Calories from Fat: 24%, Total Fat: 7g, Saturated Fat: 2g, Cholesterol: 14mg, Carbohydrate: 48g, Fiber: 1g, Protein: 2g

Banana Chocolate Cupcakes

Banana Chocolate Cupcakes

2 cups all-purpose flour
¾ cup granulated sugar, divided
¼ cup unsweetened cocoa powder
¾ teaspoon baking soda
½ teaspoon baking powder
¼ teaspoon salt
1 container (6 ounces) plain or banana-flavored low-fat yogurt
½ cup mashed ripe banana (1 medium banana)
⅓ cup vegetable oil
¼ cup fat-free (skim) milk
2 teaspoons vanilla
3 egg whites
Powdered Sugar Glaze (recipe follows)

1. Preheat oven to 350°F. Line 20 standard (2½-inch) muffin cups with paper baking cups.

2. Combine flour, ¼ cup sugar, cocoa, baking soda, baking powder and salt in large bowl. Stir yogurt, banana, oil, milk and vanilla in small bowl until well blended.

3. Beat egg whites in medium bowl with electric mixer at medium speed until foamy. Gradually add remaining ½ cup sugar, beating well after each addition, until sugar is dissolved and stiff peaks form. Stir yogurt mixture into flour mixture just until dry ingredients are moistened. Gently fold in one third of egg white mixture until blended; fold in remaining egg white mixture. Spoon evenly into prepared muffin cups, filling two-thirds full.

4. Bake 20 to 25 minutes or until toothpick inserted into centers comes out clean. Remove to wire racks; cool completely. Meanwhile, prepare Powdered Sugar Glaze; drizzle over cupcakes. Let stand until set. Store in airtight container at room temperature.

Makes 20 cupcakes

Powdered Sugar Glaze: Whisk ½ cup powdered sugar and 1 tablespoon water in small bowl until smooth; add additional water, if necessary, to reach desired consistency.

Nutrients per Serving (1 cupcake): Sodium: 109mg, Calories: 138, Calories from Fat: 26%, Total Fat: 4g, Saturated Fat: <1g, Cholesterol: 1mg, Carbohydrate: 23g, Fiber: <1g, Protein: 3g

Sour Cream Apple Tart

Sour Cream Apple Tart

5 tablespoons reduced-fat margarine, divided
¾ cup graham cracker crumbs
1¼ teaspoons ground cinnamon, divided
1⅓ cups reduced-fat sour cream
¾ cup sugar, divided
½ cup all-purpose flour, divided
½ cup cholesterol-free egg substitute
1 teaspoon vanilla
5 cups coarsely chopped peeled Jonathan apples or other firm red-skinned apples

1. Preheat oven to 350°F.

2. Melt 3 tablespoons margarine in small saucepan over medium heat. Stir in graham cracker crumbs and ¼ teaspoon cinnamon until well blended. Press crumb mixture firmly onto bottom of 9-inch springform pan. Bake 10 minutes. Cool completely.

3. Beat sour cream, ½ cup sugar and 2 tablespoons plus 1½ teaspoons flour in large bowl with electric mixer at medium speed until well blended. Beat in egg substitute and vanilla until well blended. Stir in apples. Spoon into prepared crust.

4. Bake 35 minutes or until center is just set.

5. Meanwhile, combine remaining 1 teaspoon cinnamon, ¼ cup sugar and 5 tablespoons plus 1½ teaspoons flour in small bowl. Cut in remaining 2 tablespoons margarine with pastry blender or two knives until mixture resembles coarse crumbs. Sprinkle mixture evenly over top of fruit.

6. Preheat broiler. Broil 3 to 4 minutes or until topping is golden brown. Let stand 15 minutes before slicing.   *Makes 12 servings*

Nutrients per Serving (1 slice): Sodium: 124mg, Calories: 180, Calories from Fat: 25%, Total Fat: 5g, Saturated Fat: <1g, Cholesterol: 8mg, Carbohydrate: 30g, Fiber: 1g, Protein: 3g

Mystical Layered Bars

Mystical Layered Bars

⅓ cup (⅔ stick) butter, melted
1 cup graham cracker crumbs
½ cup old-fashioned or quick oats
1 can (14 ounces) sweetened condensed milk
1 cup flaked coconut
¾ cup semisweet chocolate chips
¾ cup raisins
1 cup coarsely chopped pecans

1. Preheat oven to 350°F. Place butter in 13×9-inch baking pan, tilting to coat evenly.

2. Sprinkle graham cracker crumbs and oats evenly over butter; press with fork. Drizzle condensed milk over oats. Layer coconut, chocolate chips, raisins and pecans over milk.

3. Bake 25 to 30 minutes or until lightly browned. Cool in pan on wire rack 5 minutes; cut into 2×1½-inch bars. Cool completely in pan. Store tightly covered at room temperature or freeze up to 3 months.   *Makes 2 dozen bars*

Nutrients per Serving (1 bar): Sodium: 70mg, Calories: 180, Calories from Fat: 51%, Total Fat: 10g, Saturated Fat: 5g, Cholesterol: 10mg, Carbohydrate: 22g, Fiber: 2g, Protein: 3g

Snacks

Mediterranean Pita Pizzas

2 (8-inch) pita bread rounds
1 teaspoon olive oil
1 cup canned cannellini beans, rinsed and drained
2 teaspoons lemon juice
2 cloves garlic, minced
½ cup thinly sliced radicchio or escarole lettuce (optional)
½ cup chopped seeded tomato
½ cup finely chopped red onion
¼ cup (1 ounce) crumbled feta cheese
2 tablespoons sliced pitted black olives

1. Preheat oven to 450°F. Arrange pitas on baking sheet; brush with oil. Bake 6 minutes.

2. Meanwhile, place beans in small bowl; mash lightly with fork. Stir in lemon juice and garlic.

3. Spread bean mixture evenly on pita rounds to within ½ inch of edges. Top with radicchio, if desired, tomato, onion, cheese and olives. Bake 5 minutes or until toppings are heated through and crust is crisp. Cut each pizza into four wedges.

Makes 8 servings

Nutrients per Serving (1 wedge): Sodium: 282mg, Calories: 98, Calories from Fat: 28%, Total Fat: 3g, Saturated Fat: 1g, Cholesterol: 7mg, Carbohydrate: 14g, Fiber: 2g, Protein: 4g

Coconut Almond Biscotti

Coconut Almond Biscotti

2½ cups all-purpose flour
1⅓ cups unsweetened shredded coconut
¾ cup sliced almonds
⅔ cup sugar
2 teaspoons baking powder
½ teaspoon salt
½ cup (1 stick) light butter, melted
1 egg, at room temperature
1 egg white, at room temperature
1 teaspoon vanilla

1. Preheat oven to 350°F. Line baking sheet with parchment paper.

2. Beat flour, coconut, almonds, sugar, baking powder and salt in large bowl with electric mixer at low speed until combined.

3. Whisk butter, egg, egg white and vanilla in medium bowl. Add to dry ingredients; beat at low speed until blended.

4. Divide dough into two pieces. Dust hands lightly with flour and shape each piece into 8×2×¾-inch loaf. Place loaves on baking sheet.

5. Bake 26 to 28 minutes or until golden and set. Cool on baking sheet on wire rack 10 minutes.

6. Cut each loaf into ½-inch-thick diagonal slices with serrated knife. Place slices cut sides down on baking sheets.

7. Bake 20 minutes or until firm and golden. Remove to wire rack; cool completely. *Makes 2 dozen biscotti*

Nutrients per Serving (1 biscotti): Sodium: 68mg, Calories: 126, Calories from Fat: 43%, Total Fat: 6g, Saturated Fat: 3g, Cholesterol: 14mg, Carbohydrate: 15g, Fiber: 1g, Protein: 3g

Peppy Snack Mix

Peppy Snack Mix

3 (3-inch) plain rice cakes, broken into bite-size pieces
1½ cups bite-size frosted shredded wheat cereal
¾ cup pretzel sticks, halved
3 tablespoons reduced-fat margarine, melted
2 teaspoons reduced-sodium Worcestershire sauce
¾ teaspoon chili powder
⅛ to ¼ teaspoon ground red pepper

1. Preheat oven to 300°F. Combine rice cakes, cereal and pretzels in 13×9-inch baking pan.

2. Combine margarine, Worcestershire sauce, chili powder and red pepper in small bowl. Drizzle over cereal mixture; toss to coat.

3. Bake 20 minutes, stirring after 10 minutes.

Makes 6 servings (about 4 cups)

Nutrients per Serving (⅔ cup): Sodium: 156mg, Calories: 118, Calories from Fat: 23%, Total Fat: 3g, Saturated Fat: 1g, Cholesterol: 0mg, Carbohydrate: 20g, Fiber: 1g, Protein: 2g

Creamy Dill Cheese Spread

2 tablespoons reduced-fat cream cheese with herbs and garlic
1 tablespoon reduced-fat mayonnaise
1 tablespoon reduced-fat sour cream
1 to 2 teaspoons chopped fresh dill
⅛ teaspoon salt (optional)
24 garlic-flavored melba rounds

1. Combine cream cheese, mayonnaise, sour cream, dill and salt, if desired, in small bowl. Cover and refrigerate 1 hour.

2. To serve, top each melba round with ½ teaspoon spread.

Makes 4 servings

Nutrients per Serving (6 topped melba rounds): Sodium: 170mg, Calories: 95, Calories from Fat: 28%, Total Fat: 3g, Saturated Fat: 1g, Cholesterol: 6mg, Carbohydrate: 14g, Fiber: 1g, Protein: 2g

Trail Mix Truffles

Trail Mix Truffles

⅓ cup dried apples
¼ cup dried apricots
¼ cup apple butter
2 tablespoons golden raisins
1 tablespoon reduced-fat peanut butter
½ cup reduced-fat granola
4 tablespoons graham cracker crumbs, divided
¼ cup mini semisweet chocolate chips
1 tablespoon water

1. Combine apples, apricots, apple butter, raisins and peanut butter in food processor or blender; process until smooth. Stir in granola, 1 tablespoon graham cracker crumbs, chocolate chips and water. Shape into 16 balls.

2. Place remaining 3 tablespoons graham cracker crumbs in shallow dish; roll balls in crumbs. Cover and refrigerate until ready to serve. *Makes 8 servings*

Nutrients per Serving (2 truffles): Sodium: 14mg, Calories: 121, Calories from Fat: 30%, Total Fat: 4g, Saturated Fat: 1g, Cholesterol: 0mg, Carbohydrate: 20g, Fiber: 2g, Protein: 3g

Roasted Garlic and Spinach Spirals

Roasted Garlic and Spinach Spirals

1 whole head garlic
3 cups spinach leaves
1 can (about 15 ounces) white beans, rinsed and drained
1 teaspoon dried oregano
¼ teaspoon black pepper
⅛ teaspoon ground red pepper
7 (7-inch) flour tortillas

1. Preheat oven to 400°F. Trim top off garlic; discard. Moisten head of garlic with water; wrap in foil. Bake 45 minutes or until garlic is soft; cool completely.

2. Meanwhile, finely shred spinach leaves by stacking and cutting several leaves at a time. Place in medium bowl.

3. Remove garlic from skin and place in food processor. Add beans, oregano, black pepper and red pepper; process until smooth. Add to spinach; mix well.

4. Spread mixture evenly onto tortillas; roll up jelly-roll style. Cover and refrigerate 1 to 2 hours.

5. Trim ½ inch off ends of rolls; discard. Cut rolls into 1-inch pieces.

Makes 10 servings

Nutrients per Serving (4 spirals): Sodium: 293mg, Calories: 139, Calories from Fat: 13%, Total Fat: 2g, Saturated Fat: <1g, Cholesterol: 0mg, Carbohydrate: 25g, Fiber: 1g, Protein: 6g

Cinnamon Caramel Corn

Cinnamon Caramel Corn

8 cups air-popped popcorn (about ⅓ cup kernels)
2 tablespoons honey
4 teaspoons butter
¼ teaspoon ground cinnamon

1. Preheat oven to 350°F. Spray jelly-roll pan with nonstick cooking spray. Place popcorn in large bowl.

2. Combine honey, butter and cinnamon in small saucepan; cook and stir over low heat until butter is melted and mixture is smooth. Immediately pour over popcorn; toss to coat evenly. Spread on prepared pan.

3. Bake 12 to 14 minutes or until coating is golden brown and appears crackled, stirring twice.

4. Cool popcorn on pan. (As popcorn cools, coating becomes crisp. If not crisp enough, or if popcorn softens upon standing, return to oven and bake 5 to 8 minutes.) Store in airtight container.

Makes 4 servings (about 8 cups)

Cajun Popcorn: Preheat oven and prepare jelly-roll pan as directed above. Substitute 1 teaspoon Cajun or Creole seasoning for the cinnamon and add additional 1 teaspoon honey. Proceed as directed above.

Italian Popcorn: Spray 8 cups air-popped popcorn with fat-free butter-flavored cooking spray. Sprinkle with 2 tablespoons grated Parmesan cheese, ½ teaspoon dried oregano and ⅛ teaspoon black pepper. Gently toss to coat. Bake as directed above.

Nutrients per Serving (2 cups): Sodium: 45mg, Calories: 117, Calories from Fat: 31%, Total Fat: 4g, Saturated Fat: 1g, Cholesterol: 0mg, Carbohydrate: 19g, Fiber: 1g, Protein: 2g

Baked Apricot Brie

Baked Apricot Brie

1 round (8 ounces) Brie cheese
⅓ cup apricot preserves
2 tablespoons sliced almonds
Assorted crackers

1. Preheat oven to 400°F. Place cheese in small baking pan. Spread top of cheese with preserves; sprinkle with almonds.

2. Bake 10 to 12 minutes or until cheese begins to melt and lose its shape. Serve hot with crackers. Refrigerate leftovers.

Makes 6 servings

Note: Brie is a soft-ripened, unpressed cheese made from cow's milk. It has a distinctive round shape, edible white rind and creamy yellow interior. Avoid Brie that has a chalky center (it is underripe) or a strong ammonia odor (it is overripe). The cheese should give slightly to pressure and have an evenly colored, barely moist rind.

Nutrients per Serving (⅙ of total recipe): Sodium: 239mg, Calories: 189, Calories from Fat: 57%, Total Fat: 12g, Saturated Fat: 7g, Cholesterol: 37mg, Carbohydrate: 13g, Fiber: <1g, Protein: 8g

Herbed Potato Chips

Herbed Potato Chips

    Nonstick cooking spray
 2 unpeeled medium red potatoes (about ½ pound)
 1 tablespoon olive oil
 2 tablespoons minced fresh dill, thyme or rosemary *or*
    2 teaspoons dried dill weed, thyme or rosemary
 ¼ teaspoon garlic salt
 ⅛ teaspoon black pepper
 1¼ cups fat-free sour cream

1. Preheat oven to 450°F. Spray baking sheets with cooking spray.

2. Cut potatoes crosswise into very thin slices, about ¹⁄₁₆ inch thick. Pat dry with paper towels. Arrange potato slices in single layer on prepared baking sheets; spray with cooking spray.

3. Bake 10 minutes; turn slices over. Brush with oil. Combine dill, garlic salt and pepper in small bowl; sprinkle evenly over potato slices.

4. Bake 5 to 10 minutes or until golden brown. Cool on baking sheets. Serve with sour cream.   *Makes 6 servings*

Nutrients per Serving (10 chips with about 3 tablespoons sour cream): Sodium: 84mg, Calories: 106, Calories from Fat: 17%, Total Fat: 2g, Saturated Fat: <1g, Cholesterol: 8mg, Carbohydrate: 16g, Fiber: 1g, Protein: 4g

Wild Wedges

Wild Wedges

2 (8-inch) fat-free flour tortillas
   Nonstick cooking spray
⅓ cup shredded reduced-fat Cheddar cheese
⅓ cup chopped cooked chicken or turkey
   1 green onion, thinly sliced
2 tablespoons mild thick and chunky salsa

1. Heat large nonstick skillet over medium heat. Spray one tortilla with cooking spray; place in skillet, sprayed side down. Top with cheese, chicken, green onion and salsa. Place remaining tortilla over mixture; spray with cooking spray.

2. Cook 2 to 3 minutes per side or until golden brown and cheese is melted. Cut into eight wedges. *Makes 4 servings*

Variation: For bean quesadillas, omit the chicken and substitute with ⅓ cup canned fat-free refried beans.

Nutrients per Serving (2 wedges): Sodium: 224mg, Calories: 82, Calories from Fat: 22%, Total Fat: 2g, Saturated Fat: 1g, Cholesterol: 13mg, Carbohydrate: 8g, Fiber: 3g, Protein: 7g

Dilly Deviled Eggs

Dilly Deviled Eggs

6 hard-cooked eggs, peeled and sliced in half lengthwise
1 tablespoon reduced-fat sour cream
1 tablespoon low-fat mayonnaise
1 tablespoon low-fat (1%) cottage cheese
1 tablespoon minced fresh dill *or* **1 teaspoon dried dill weed**
1 tablespoon minced dill pickle
1 teaspoon Dijon mustard
⅛ teaspoon salt
⅛ teaspoon white pepper
  Paprika (optional)
  Dill sprigs (optional)

1. Remove yolks from egg halves; place in small bowl. Add sour cream, mayonnaise, cottage cheese, minced dill, pickle, mustard, salt and white pepper; mash with fork.

2. Fill egg halves with mixture using teaspoon or piping bag fitted with large, plain tip. Garnish filled egg halves with paprika and dill sprigs, if desired. *Makes 6 servings*

Nutrients per Serving (2 egg halves): Sodium: 177mg, Calories: 93, Calories from Fat: 58% Total Fat: 6g, Saturated Fat: 2g, Cholesterol: 214mg, Carbohydrate: 1g, Fiber: <1g, Protein: 7g

Peanut Butter Cereal Bars

Peanut Butter Cereal Bars

3 cups mini marshmallows
3 tablespoons butter or margarine
½ cup reduced-fat peanut butter
3½ cups crisp rice cereal
1 cup quick oats
⅓ cup mini semisweet chocolate chips

Microwave Directions

1. Spray 13×9-inch baking pan with nonstick cooking spray.

2. Combine marshmallows and butter in large microwavable bowl. Microwave on HIGH 15 seconds; stir. Microwave 1 minute; stir until marshmallows are melted and mixture is smooth. Add peanut butter; stir. Add cereal and oats; stir until well coated. Spread into prepared pan. Immediately sprinkle with chocolate chips, pressing chips lightly into cereal mixture.

3. Cool completely in pan. Cut into 40 bars to serve.

Makes 40 servings

Tip: To reduce sticking, spray your spoon with nonstick cooking spray before stirring in the cereal. Spray the spoon again before spreading the mixture in the pan.

Nutrients per Serving (1 bar): Sodium: 54mg, Calories: 66, Calories from Fat: 41%, Total Fat: 3g, Saturated Fat: 1g, Cholesterol: 2mg, Carbohydrate: 10g, Fiber: 1g, Protein: 1g

METRIC CONVERSION CHART

VOLUME MEASUREMENTS (dry)

$^1/_8$ teaspoon = 0.5 mL
$^1/_4$ teaspoon = 1 mL
$^1/_2$ teaspoon = 2 mL
$^3/_4$ teaspoon = 4 mL
1 teaspoon = 5 mL
1 tablespoon = 15 mL
2 tablespoons = 30 mL
$^1/_4$ cup = 60 mL
$^1/_3$ cup = 75 mL
$^1/_2$ cup = 125 mL
$^2/_3$ cup = 150 mL
$^3/_4$ cup = 175 mL
1 cup = 250 mL
2 cups = 1 pint = 500 mL
3 cups = 750 mL
4 cups = 1 quart = 1 L

VOLUME MEASUREMENTS (fluid)

1 fluid ounce (2 tablespoons) = 30 mL
4 fluid ounces ($^1/_2$ cup) = 125 mL
8 fluid ounces (1 cup) = 250 mL
12 fluid ounces ($1^1/_2$ cups) = 375 mL
16 fluid ounces (2 cups) = 500 mL

WEIGHTS (mass)

$^1/_2$ ounce = 15 g
1 ounce = 30 g
3 ounces = 90 g
4 ounces = 120 g
8 ounces = 225 g
10 ounces = 285 g
12 ounces = 360 g
16 ounces = 1 pound = 450 g

DIMENSIONS

$^1/_{16}$ inch = 2 mm
$^1/_8$ inch = 3 mm
$^1/_4$ inch = 6 mm
$^1/_2$ inch = 1.5 cm
$^3/_4$ inch = 2 cm
1 inch = 2.5 cm

OVEN TEMPERATURES

250°F = 120°C
275°F = 140°C
300°F = 150°C
325°F = 160°C
350°F = 180°C
375°F = 190°C
400°F = 200°C
425°F = 220°C
450°F = 230°C

BAKING PAN SIZES

Utensil	Size in Inches/Quarts	Metric Volume	Size in Centimeters
Baking or Cake Pan (square or rectangular)	8×8×2	2 L	20×20×5
	9×9×2	2.5 L	23×23×5
	12×8×2	3 L	30×20×5
	13×9×2	3.5 L	33×23×5
Loaf Pan	8×4×3	1.5 L	20×10×7
	9×5×3	2 L	23×13×7
Round Layer Cake Pan	8×1½	1.2 L	20×4
	9×1½	1.5 L	23×4
Pie Plate	8×1¼	750 mL	20×3
	9×1¼	1 L	23×3
Baking Dish or Casserole	1 quart	1 L	—
	1½ quart	1.5 L	—
	2 quart	2 L	—